T0327846

BEYONCÉ
IS LIFE

A Superfan's Guide to
All Things We Love about Beyoncé

KATHLEEN PERRICONE

ILLUSTRATED BY KELLY SMITH

CONTENTS

INTRODUCTION

All hail the Queen!

Beyoncé's crown wasn't inherited; it was earned. One of the best-selling and most decorated music artists of all time, she is a multi-hyphenate who has globally impacted fashion, film, business, politics, economics, philanthropy, and culture as a whole. And that's one of the things she's most proud of—aside from being the mother of Blue, Rumi, and Sir, her three children with husband Jay-Z. "Commercial success certainly doesn't equate to being impactful," Queen Bey explained to British *Vogue*. "Cultural currency is invaluable."

Bey broke out as a solo artist at the turn of the millennium, a time when pop stars were not meant to be truly heard. Still, she raised her voice, especially as critics questioned her credibility without Destiny's Child, one of the greatest girl groups of all time. "I've been born to do this," she insisted to NBC News in 2003, while promoting her debut album *Dangerously in Love*. "I want to be a triple threat, you know? I'm able to dance, sing, act, and I also write and produce. And that's very rare. They want to say it's because of the sexy clothes or it's because whatever else. No, it's because I'm talented. And I just want to be acknowledged for that."

"I want to be a triple threat, you know? I'm able to dance, sing, act, and I also write and produce."

With each record-breaking album, Beyoncé has indeed gained greater recognition—shattering the music industry's glass ceiling in the process. In 2013, she dropped the self-titled *Beyoncé* without warning, popularizing the concept of not only a "surprise album," but also a "visual album," as each song is accompanied by a video. That year, she was hailed by *Time* magazine as "the embodiment of modern feminism." She pushed the boundaries even further, exploring Black feminism in 2016's *Lemonade*, widely considered to be one of the greatest albums of all time. Her sixth solo effort also showcased the evolution of her sound, with Grammy nominations in four distinct categories: pop, rock, rap, and urban contemporary. The Recording Academy's leading talent, with thirty-two awards, more than any other artist, Bey made her mark on the dance/electronic genre with wins for 2022's *Renaissance*. Two years later, *Cowboy Carter*'s "Texas Hold 'Em" became the first country song by a Black woman to top the *Billboard Hot 100*.

Now in the third decade of her career, the wife and mother has found the work-life balance she's always craved. In 2023, her husband and three children came along for the Renaissance World Tour, which grossed $500 million—the highest amount ever for a Black artist and the second highest for a female artist. It's her intention to keep the public's focus off her private life, while remaining connected to her BeyHive, "because if my art isn't strong enough or meaningful enough to keep people interested and inspired, then I'm in the wrong business," Beyoncé admitted to *Harper's Bazaar*. "My music, my films, my art, my message—that should be enough."

PART ONE

Rise of
a Queen

A SUPERSTAR
IS BORN

One of Beyoncé Knowles's earliest memories is sitting in her family's Houston, Texas, kitchen while her mother washed dishes. "What did you learn at school today?" asked Tina, a hair salon owner. "A song," replied the first grader. Tina stopped what she was doing, wiped her hands on her apron, and turned around to face her daughter: "Let's hear it." Over a decade later, the moment remained fresh in Bey's mind.

"I stood up to sing it for her just like my teacher had taught me," she recalled in *Soul Survivors: The Official Autobiography of Destiny's Child* (Harper Entertainment, 2002). "I'll never forget that feeling. I loved performing for my mom—it was a rush."

Long before their eldest daughter, Beyoncé Giselle, was born on September 4, 1981, Mathew and Tina Knowles filled their home with music. As teenagers, they each performed with local singing groups (with Tina as a member of The Beltones, which was modeled after The Supremes). As parents, the couple serenaded Beyoncé and her younger sister Solange and spun records by their favorite artists: Michael Jackson, Anita Baker, Luther Vandross, and Prince. "My dad tells me that as a baby, I would go crazy whenever I heard music," Bey shared in *Soul Survivors*. At the age of five, she attended her first concert—Michael Jackson's Bad World Tour—"and that night, I decided exactly my purpose," she revealed in a 2011 interview with Australian music host Molly Meldrum.

In home videos from her childhood, the little girl hams it up for the camcorder, dancing and singing made-up lyrics. But at school, she was overwhelmingly shy, to the extent that she would pretend not to hear classmates when they talked to her. Hoping to get the seven-year-old to come out of her shell, Mathew and Tina enrolled her in dance classes at a local studio operated by Darlette Johnson. "You would ask her, 'What's your name?' . . . you could barely hear her speak," Johnson recalled to CNN in 2013. But on the dance floor, "she became a different person," moving so fiercely that pieces of her costume would fly off. One day after class, Beyoncé overheard her teacher humming Lisa Stansfield's "All Around the World" and sang along. "It blew me away," said Johnson, who bribed the

*"All I know is that I felt
at home on that stage,
more so than anywhere else."*

bashful girl with a dollar to do it again. "I was floored. When her parents
came to pick her up, I told them, 'She can sing! She can really sing!'"

At Johnson's urging, Beyoncé entered a school talent show and
performed one of her favorite songs: "Imagine" by John Lennon. "It was
the first time I had ever walked on stage in front of an audience," she noted
in *Soul Survivors*. "I looked into the crowd and saw teachers, my classmates,
and their parents, fanning themselves with the paper programs and trying
to get comfortable in their yellow plastic chairs. Then I started to sing. My
parents were shocked. I can still see the looks on their faces—their mouths
dropped open in amazement. I'm not even sure where I found the courage.
All I know is that I felt at home on that stage, more so than anywhere else."
And that confidence translated to her performance: Beyoncé received a
standing ovation . . . and the winner's trophy.

In 1988, she enrolled in vocal lessons to refine her natural talent. Out on the local competition circuit, she blew away all her contenders: within two years, Beyoncé had won thirty pageants. A tomboy who preferred baggy shirts and jeans to frilly dresses, she tolerated the "beauty" requirement of contests for the chance to perform for an audience. Looking back, Bey admitted she felt uncomfortable parading around on stage in makeup and teased hair—but the trophies and crowns were a worthy consolation prize.

Two decades later, she confronted the past in the music video for 2013's "Pretty Hurts," which depicts adult Beyoncé as an aspiring pageant queen struggling with body image and "training myself to be this champion," she explained in *Self-Titled: Imperfection*, a video series about the making of her fifth album, *Beyoncé*. "At the end of the day . . . Is it worth it?" she wondered. "The trophy represents all of the sacrifices I made as a kid, all of the time that I lost." The video ends in a chilling cathartic release: Beyoncé, in a replica of her childhood bedroom, screaming as she destroys the trophy collection she once treasured.

A STAR IS REINCARNATED

Of Beyoncé's many musical influences, two had a special connection: Barbra Streisand and Judy Garland both starred in remakes of one of her favorite movies, *A Star Is Born*. In 2011, when Clint Eastwood signed on to direct the fourth adaptation, it was announced that Beyoncé would follow in the footsteps of her idols Garland and Streisand. "Every twenty to thirty years, a new star is born and a new talent represents that generation and era," she gushed to Reuters. "I didn't think that I would ever get the opportunity to be the star." But just one month after the announcement of her casting, the singer revealed she was pregnant with her first child, prompting Eastwood to shift focus to another project. A year later, Bey officially dropped out of *A Star Is Born*—which was ultimately made with Lady Gaga and Bradley Cooper in 2018.

SHE'S THAT GIRL

In 1990, as the little girl with the big voice made a name for herself around Houston, buzz about Beyoncé Knowles made its way to Deborah Laday and Denise Seals, two local talent scouts who were forming an all-female singing group, Girl's Tyme, modeled after R&B chart-toppers Boyz II Men. The nine-year-old aced her audition, beating out dozens of other hopefuls for a spot in the six-piece, which included Kelly Rowland, LaTavia Roberson, Ashley Davis, and LaTavia's cousins, sisters Nikki and Nina Taylor.

Boyz II Men had been an overnight sensation, but for the girl group it would take a little more time. Every day after school, they gathered at the Knowles' house to rehearse under the direction of Bey's father, Mathew, who took on the role of comanaging Girl's Tyme. When they weren't working on vocal harmonies or dance routines, the preteens studied the acts they hoped to emulate, watching performance videos of the Jackson 5 and The Supremes. They showed off what they had learned for a reluctant audience at Tina's hair salon. "The customers sometimes didn't want to listen," Bey's mother recalled to *Texas Monthly*. "The girls would call out, 'Put your hands together!' Customers would be rolling their eyes. That was a tough audience."

Girl's Tyme kept at it, and before long they were getting booked by people who *actually* wanted to hear them sing, with gigs consisting of birthday parties, banquets, and most notably, the Miss Black Houston Metroplex Pageant. As the group's rehearsal schedule ramped up, the daily shuttling to and from the Knowles' residence proved tricky for Kelly, whose single mother worked as a live-in nanny. "My mom asked Tina, 'Could Kelly stay with you for the summer?' And the summer turned into . . . how long?" Kelly later explained to *Interview* magazine, amid rumors she had been adopted by Beyoncé's parents. "It was like a big ol' happy family because my mom came over every night to kiss me goodnight." And although the Knowles house had six bedrooms, Kelly bunked with her close friend. "We were sleeping in the same bed, waking up every morning, singing all day, and loving every minute of it," Beyoncé reminisced to *Blender*.

In 1992, Girl's Tyme caught the ear of San Francisco music producer Arne Frager, who traveled to Houston just to watch them perform. Frager liked what he saw and flew the group out to The Plant, a recording studio made famous by the Rolling Stones, Fleetwood Mac, Stevie Wonder, John Lennon, and Prince. Girl's Tyme cut fifteen songs with Frager; however, his connection failed to generate interest from record labels. But he was able to pull some strings and get their audition tape to *Star Search*, the nationally syndicated talent competition hosted by Ed McMahon that had already discovered the likes of Britney Spears, Christina Aguilera, Aaliyah, and Usher.

It was a make-or-break opportunity, and Girl's Tyme spent months rehearsing for their two minutes on television, right down to their stage costumes (purple, lime, and white windbreakers). Led by eleven-year-old Beyoncé, the youngsters performed their little hearts out, yet when the votes were tallied, the hip-hop challengers received three stars—not enough to defeat the reigning champion, Skeleton Key, a rock band whose members were more than twice their age. "When they cut to a commercial, we ran backstage and burst into tears," Kelly recalled in *Soul Survivors*. "We almost went crazy from crying—a lot was riding on that performance," added Beyoncé.

There was a silver lining to their palpable heartbreak, however: Her father saw how badly they wanted to get to the next level and decided to step up as the group's full-time manager (co-manager Andretta Tillman was dealing with health issues at the time). Mathew quit his six-figure sales job and enrolled in an artist's management class at Houston Community College. But when he submitted their demo to record labels, the feedback was often the same: Girl's Tyme had too many members. The six were whittled down to four with the release of Nikki and Nina, who were more skilled as dancers than singers. As the group headed in its new direction, Ashley chose to focus on school instead—leaving Beyoncé, Kelly, and LaTavia to remain as the core group. A round of auditions discovered Girl's Tyme's fourth voice, LeToya Luckett.

*"We had to make up
our own games,
but we made sure we had fun."*

During the summers, Mathew put the girls through "boot camp." Each day began with a quick breakfast, then a three-hour jog while singing, to fine-tune their ability to perform without getting winded. Back at home base, the Knowles' residence, there were voice lessons, dance rehearsals, and media training. When school resumed in the fall, group practice moved to the evenings, with performances on the weekends. As their focus narrowed and a record deal felt within reach, the four girls left school ahead of tenth grade and hired full-time tutors. "Everybody else was outside playing and we were working," Kelly told the Associated Press in 1998. "But we still played. We had to make up our own games, but we made sure we had fun."

All the years of sacrifice seemed to finally pay off in 1995 when they inked a deal with Elektra Records. Yet for two years, Girl's Tyme was left to languish with a major label that didn't know exactly what to do with them. When the group was ultimately dropped in 1997, Beyoncé recalled, "It was like *Star Search* all over again."

IN GOD'S NAME

After signing with Elektra Records, Girl's Tyme signaled their next chapter with a new, mature name. The group first came up with the name Cliché, simply because they liked how the word sounded, but as its definition implies unoriginality, they moved on to something more authentic: The Dolls, "because we were like dolls come to life," Bey explained in *Soul Survivors*. "But that name was worse than Cliché." Her mother, Tina, suggested Destiny after coming across it in the Bible's book of Isaiah. Six months later, Destiny learned there were "about a hundred" other groups with the same name. Mathew came up with the idea of adding "Child" to mean a rebirth of Destiny. "People said, 'Why not Destiny's Children, since there are four of y'all?'" Bey recalled in the group's 2002 book. "And we said, 'No, it's going to be Child because we are a group that represents one person.'"

MANIFESTING
DESTINY

J ust when Beyoncé and the girls were ready to give up, opportunity knocked. Columbia Records offered Destiny's Child a deal in 1997, and that October their debut single, "No, No, No," was received by music fans with a "Yes, Yes, Yes." Within two years, their breakthrough sophomore album, *The Writing's on the Wall*, spawned the No. 1 singles "Bills, Bills, Bills" and "Say My Name," and, perhaps unbelievably, two Grammys. However, when Destiny's Child stepped onstage to accept their first trophy at the 2001 awards ceremony, they were a trio: Beyoncé, Kelly . . . and Michelle Williams.

The year prior, as Destiny's Child was skyrocketing to fame, LaTavia and LeToya attempted to remove Mathew as their manager. Although they intended to remain in the group, the writing was on the wall and the duo was privately dismissed. Weeks later, when the video for "Say My Name" premiered on MTV, fans got their first look at the two new members of Destiny's Child, Michelle Williams and Farrah Franklin. The swap was just as confusing to LaTavia and LeToya, who filed a lawsuit against Mathew for breach of partnership. As Beyoncé and Kelly moved forward with Michelle and Farrah, they couldn't help but notice that Farrah didn't seem as interested. She kept to herself, never spoke in meetings, and skipped out on several rehearsals. Then, in the middle of a promotional trip, she left a note saying she had flown home to Los Angeles. With a sold-out Australian tour just days away, Beyoncé called Farrah (using Michelle's cell phone) to convince her to rejoin the group, but she refused to get on the plane. "If you could have seen the look on Beyoncé's face," Kelly recounted in *Soul Survivors*. It was the last straw. As Michelle remembered it, Bey ended the conversation with, "Well, then I wish you the best. May God bless you. Goodbye!"

As a trio, Destiny's Child hit all the right notes. The official debut of Beyoncé, Kelly, and Michelle remains iconic: "Independent Women, Part 1," the theme song for the 2000 film *Charlie's Angels* starring Drew Barrymore, Cameron Diaz, and Lucy Liu. Between the empowering lyrics and the butt-kicking video, the anthem established the trio as a triumvirate, no longer gossip fodder for the music industry. They had made it through the firestorm—and had come out stronger than ever, as they proved on their appropriately titled third album, *Survivor*. Beyoncé cowrote and coproduced the title track, which includes a lyric straight out of her

*They had made it
through the firestorm —
and had come out
stronger than ever.*

final conversation with Farrah as Beyoncé wishes her the best, success, and happiness. The song wasn't directed at anyone in particular, insisted Beyoncé. "I thought about this joke that this radio station had, and they were saying, 'Oh, Destiny's Child is like [the CBS reality competition show] *Survivor*, trying to see which member is going to last the longest on the island,' and everyone laughed," she told MTV News. "I was like, 'Ah, that's cute, but you know what? I'm going to use that negative thing and turn it into a positive thing and try to write a great song out of it.'"

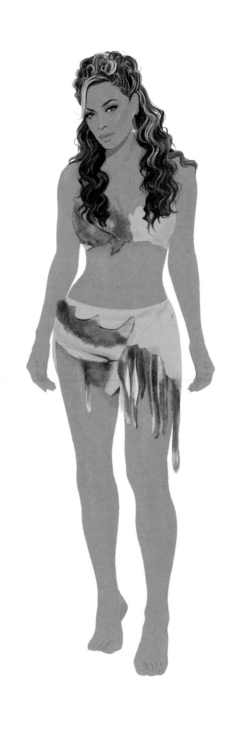

With twelve million album copies sold worldwide, Destiny's Child had silenced their skeptics. Yet, Beyoncé remained a lightning rod for criticism. According to the rumor mill, she was a spotlight-stealing egomaniac whose songwriting talents were highly exaggerated. "I hear all the things people say and sometimes I just can't take it," the twenty-year-old admitted to the *Los Angeles Times* in 2001. "It's crazy. It drives you crazy if you listen." There were also whispers about Beyoncé leaving the group to embark on a solo career, but the truth was that each singer planned to do her own thing—albeit for the greater good of Destiny's Child.

"We are negotiating solo projects for all three of us," Beyoncé clarified amid reports she had already inked a three-record deal. "They're all going to come out at the same time. We're going to all do different types of music and support each other's albums. Basically, they're not going to compete with each other. And we'll come back and do another album for Destiny's Child, and hopefully, it will broaden our audience, so it will help us all out."

In December 2001, the trio announced a temporary hiatus as they independently concentrated on new music. Michelle was the first to release a solo album, *Heart to Yours*, which went all the way to No. 1 on the *Billboard* Top Gospel Albums chart in April 2002. Five months later, Kelly was next with the R&B-pop-rock album *Simply Deep*. Last but not least, Beyoncé dropped *Dangerously in Love,* which sold three times as much as the other two albums combined in its first week in June 2003. Still, she was emphatic her success did not spell the end of Destiny's Child. "We haven't broken up," she told Australia's *Thread*. "We're going to continue to tour and record and be a group."

As promised, Beyoncé, Kelly, and Michelle reunited as Destiny's Child in 2004. But the title of their fifth album suggested it would be their last: *Destiny Fulfilled*. When asked, their lips were sealed—and the trio's body language suggested they were as tight as ever. "Who knows what will happen in three, five, or ten years?" Beyoncé mused to *Billboard*. "The main thing is that we maintain our friendship and that we do it because we want to—not because it's a good business move." Months later, however, they laid the rumors to rest with the announcement that they were "to leave Destiny's Child on a high note, united in our friendship and filled with an overwhelming gratitude for our music, our fans, and each other." There was no denying they had fulfilled their destinies: with sixty million albums sold, they remain one of the most successful girl groups in history.

To the other members of Destiny's Child, the Knowleses became a second family. Kelly, who didn't know her father growing up, considered Mathew a paternal figure and even called him "Dad." Michelle credited "wonderful" Tina with her style evolution, which unlocked her confidence and "helped me to discover another side of my personality," she wrote in *Soul Survivors*. "I never could have done it without the support of Miss Tina and the group."

FAMILY AFFAIR

In order for their daughter to realize her dreams, Beyoncé's parents sacrificed everything. Mathew quit his job to manage their daughter, while Tina worked extra hours at her hair salon to pay the bills—which climbed to the hundreds of thousands while promoting the girl group. As debt piled up, the couple was forced to sell their home, and eventually, they separated. But once Destiny's Child achieved stardom, success helped mend the fractured Knowles family, who all joined Bey on the journey. Mathew continued to manage the group, while Tina came on as their stylist and created their iconic matching looks. Little sister Solange, also a talented singer, was recruited as a backup dancer. "We've gotten to see the world together," Mathew gushed to MTV News. "The traveling and the experiences that we've had, it's been really, really a wonderful, wonderful thing."

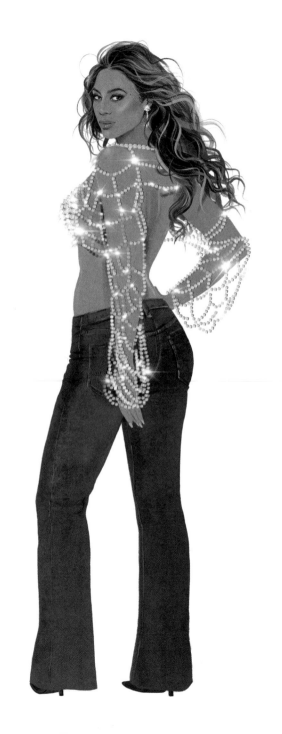

INDEPENDENT
WOMAN

Since she was nine years old, Beyoncé had been part of a group. Embarking on a solo career at the age of twenty-one conjured a roller coaster of emotions, including a brief period of depression. For more than a decade, Kelly had been by her side "every day of my life, every time I've been on a stage, every interview," Beyoncé told *Time* in 2003. "So, it makes me nervous she's not here. But it's a necessary challenge because I'm an adult. We're all adults now, and we need to learn things about ourselves, and sometimes you can't do that unless you're by yourself."

"I wanna be remembered and I wanna be respected. And I wanna be an icon."

As one-third of Destiny's Child, Beyoncé was a rising star. As a solo artist, she quickly became one of the biggest superstars on the planet. Within two years of her debut album *Dangerously in Love*, she had won five Grammys, sang the National Anthem at the Super Bowl, inked multimillion-dollar endorsement deals with Pepsi and Tommy Hilfiger, landed the cover of *Rolling Stone*, and been cast in three Hollywood films. As she looked ahead to her second solo album—and beyond—she mused to *The Face* magazine, "I wanna be remembered and I wanna be respected. And I wanna be an icon."

The stakes were higher for her 2006 follow-up, *B'Day*, released a year after Destiny's Child officially disbanded. There would be no going back, as Beyoncé certified her global domination, topping the charts throughout Europe, South America, Japan, and Australia. Not only did she collaborate with Queen of Latin Music Shakira on "Beautiful Liar"—which reached No. 1 in fifteen countries—she recorded Spanish-language versions of several *B'Day* tracks, plus "Amor Gitano" ("Gypsy Love") with Mexican singer Alejandro Fernández, for the four-song EP *Irreemplazable (Irreplaceable)*.

Fans got double the Beyoncé in 2008 when she introduced her alter ego for her third album, the "too aggressive, too strong, too sassy, too sexy" Sasha Fierce. It was a risky gimmick. Historically in pop culture, fictional counterparts are polarizing—for every Ziggy Stardust (David Bowie's alien counterpart), there's a Chris Gaines (Garth Brooks's widely lampooned rockstar persona). But Bey beat the odds: *I Am . . . Sasha Fierce* ranked as one of the best albums of the 2000s, and more than fifteen years later social media is still flooded with daily mentions of Sasha Fierce.

Once she wrapped the exhaustive I Am . . . World Tour in 2010, Beyoncé heeded her mother's advice to "live your life and open your eyes"—and during a year-long hiatus, she took a closer look at her career. When she shifted back to work mode for her fourth album, *4*, Bey made the decision to part ways professionally with her father Mathew and establish her own management company, Parkwood Entertainment. "It's very difficult managing myself," she admitted in the MTV special, *Year of 4*. "Every night when I go to sleep, I ask hundreds of questions. I'm making mistakes, and I'm learning from them . . . I'm learning to drown out the noise. I only have to follow my heart. I run my world," she concluded, in a nod to *4*'s hit single, "Run the World (Girls)."

Emboldened by her own independence, Bey made feminism a central theme of 2013's *Beyoncé*—a surprise, visual album that brought each track to life with its own music video. In "***Flawless" and "Pretty Hurts," she especially explored gender inequality. "Equality is a myth," she declared in the accompanying documentary *Life Is But a Dream*, "and for some reason, everyone accepts the fact that women don't make as much money as men do. I don't understand that. Why do we have to take a backseat? I truly believe that women should be financially independent from their men. And let's face it, money gives men the power to run the show. It gives men the power to define value. They define what's sexy. And men define what's feminine. It's ridiculous."

Beyoncé redefined her legacy with 2016's *Lemonade*, an artistically intimate glimpse into how she processed infidelity in her marriage with Jay-Z by healing generational trauma within her extended family. Widely credited as her landmark album, its title alludes to making the best of a bad situation. And as she learned, some of the "lemons" life threw at her ultimately resulted in the sweetest lemonade. "All pain and loss are, in fact, a gift," Bey explained to *Elle*. "I died and was reborn in my relationship, and the quest for self became even stronger. It's difficult for me to go backward. Being 'number one' was no longer my priority. My true win is creating art and a legacy that will live far beyond me. That's fulfilling."

Two decades after her solo debut—and practically a lifetime as a performer—Beyoncé set out to share music's healing powers as the world emerged from the devastating coronavirus pandemic. In 2020, she began recording her seventh album, *Renaissance*—a light in the darkness of the time. "My intention was to create a safe place, a place without judgment," she explained to fans in 2022. "A place to be free of perfectionism and overthinking. A place to scream, release, feel freedom." Beyoncé recreated that vibe night after night on the 2023 Renaissance Tour, a cultural phenomenon that swept the globe: From Stockholm to St. Louis, an estimated three million people entered the House of Chrome dressed to the nines in silver fashions, hoping to forget about their troubles for a few hours. "We'll surround ourselves in a shimmering human disco ball each night," encouraged Bey on Instagram. "Everybody mirroring each other's joy."

The year 2023 brought a reunion so epic it was twenty-three years in the making: Former Destiny's Child members LaTavia Roberson and LeToya Luckett attended the Renaissance Tour's stop in Houston—and met up with Beyoncé, Kelly, and Michelle backstage. Dubbed "DC5" by fans, it was the first time the women had ever been in the same room together, and it was captured by cameras for Bey's *Renaissance* concert film. At the Los Angeles premiere, "DC5" had a second reunion when Kelly, Michelle, LaTavia, and LeToya all hit the red carpet in support of Beyoncé. "Love, love, love is what was in that room," LeToya gushed on *The Grape Juice* podcast in January 2024. "That was a remarkable experience."

SOUL SISTERS

The moment Destiny's Child split, there was already talk about reuniting in the future. "It's not smart to say 'never,'" Beyoncé teased in 2005, during their first interview since the news broke. "It's not the end." Sure enough, two years later Kelly and Michelle made cameos in her "Get Me Bodied" video and surprised fans in Los Angeles by singing "Happy Birthday" to the star during a stop on her tour, The Beyoncé Experience. But it wasn't until 2013 that the BeyHive got their wish: an official Destiny's Child reunion at Beyoncé's Super Bowl Halftime Show. Seven minutes into the performance, Kelly and Michelle popped up from beneath the stage (literally!) for a medley of "Bootylicious" and "Independent Women, Part I." As the music segued into "Single Ladies," Bey asked, "Kelly, Michelle, can ya'll help me sing this one?" They sure did, each taking a line for their own solo moment, as Beyoncé shared the biggest night of her career with two people who helped her get there. Five years later, they did it again for her next milestone, headlining 2018's Coachella.

LOVE ON TOP

Beyoncé's first love has been her one and only for over two decades. She was a teenage pop star when she crossed paths with Jay-Z in Cancun, Mexico, at a taping of *MTV Spring Break* in 2000. The rapper recounted the fateful moment in his 2018 track "713" (the area code for Houston, Bey's hometown): Both artists were there to perform at the Fashionably Loud concert, but they "played it cool at the pool." On the flight home, who else was seated next to him but Beyoncé, "and I knew straight away." It would be another two years before they actually went on their first date, dinner at sushi hotspot Nobu.

Rumors ignited about two of the biggest names in music when Bey popped up on Jay's track "'03 Bonnie & Clyde"—and the lyrics sounded suspiciously autobiographical, with the artists referring to each other as boyfriend and girlfriend and making grand declarations of love "until the very end." The cinematic video was Jay's fantasy come to life. Based on one of his favorite movies, *True Romance*, starring Christian Slater and Patricia Arquette as newlyweds on the run from drug dealers, "'03 Bonnie & Clyde" oozes with chemistry between the couple (who avoided the same fate as the real-life Bonnie Parker and Clyde Barrow, bank robbers who were shot and killed by police in 1934). The storyline continued in the video for Beyoncé's debut solo single, "Crazy in Love," featuring Jay-Z rapping in front of a burning car as his girlfriend shimmies around him. Was art imitating life? Any time a reporter asked, the singer bashfully declined to comment—until she sat down with Oprah Winfrey. In a 2003 appearance on Oprah's daytime talk show, Beyoncé confirmed the relationship and explained why she kept it private. "I think it's important that I concentrate on the music, and when you start talking about those things, then that becomes bigger than the art."

True to her words, Beyoncé rarely spoke publicly about Jay-Z—even their April 2008 wedding was a well-kept secret, with only thirty people invited to the intimate ceremony inside their Manhattan penthouse. She was equally tight-lipped about their plans to start a family. When Bey was finally pregnant, she uncharacteristically announced it onstage at the 2011 *MTV Video Music Awards* by unbuttoning her sequined blazer and rubbing her growing belly. But as conspiracy theories swirled that Beyoncé was faking it with a prosthetic belly, she retreated from the public eye until welcoming daughter Blue Ivy on January 7, 2012. It was "the best day of

"I felt it was important to uplift and praise our boys . . ."

my life," the new mom gushed to *Vogue*. "She's my homey, my best friend."
Five years later, the family of three grew by two when Beyoncé gave birth
to twins, daughter Rumi (after her favorite poet) and son Sir, whose entry
into the world inspired his unique name. "Sir was like, man, come out the
gate," Jay-Z revealed in a *Tidal* interview. "He just came out, like, Sir."

Motherhood has been Beyoncé's biggest inspiration, and she's
applied it to every aspect of her work. After a family trip to South Africa,
she came up with the idea for *Black Is King*—a musical film about an exiled
African prince to accompany *The Lion King: The Gift* soundtrack—which she
dedicated to Sir. "I felt it was important to uplift and praise our boys and
to assure that they grow up with enough films, children's books, and music
that promote emotional intelligence, self-value, and our rich history," she
told *Vogue* in 2020. Blue and Rumi appear in the visual for "Brown Skin
Girl," a song the elder sister wrote with their mother. The children also
influenced Beyoncé's fashion line, Ivy Park. In 2021, she dropped the first

*"Look what it's done
to the culture.
Look how the energy
of the world moved."*

kids' collection, a mini-me version of the adult styles, because "we love to coordinate our outfits" as a family.

When Beyoncé returned in 2022 with her first album in six years, *Renaissance*, she gave a special shoutout to the four people who made it possible: "Rumi, Sir, and Blue for allowing me the space, creativity, and inspiration. And a special thanks to my husband and muse, who held me down during those late nights in the studio." The whole family hit the road for the 2023 Renaissance World Tour, and Jay-Z was regularly spotted in the audience, cheering on his wife along with tens of thousands of fans. At the Paris concert, he had another reason to be proud: Blue, eleven, joined Beyoncé onstage as a backup dancer for several songs. The moment gave him goosebumps, he gushed to Gayle King on *CBS Mornings*. "She wanted to do it the first night, and we was like, 'OK, if this is something you want to do, you can't just go out there. You gotta go work with the dancers and go work.'" Blue rehearsed so much, some days she had to ice her sore back. But for the seventh show, she was ready.

The *Renaissance* concert film gave a behind-the-scenes peek at the private discussions leading up to the moment. "I did not think it was an appropriate place for an eleven-year-old on the stadium stage," Beyoncé admitted. "All of the things I've had to go through, the obstacles I've had to overcome, prepared me. She hasn't had that struggle." Blue's performance lit up social media, but amid the overwhelming support from fans, there were scrutinizing trolls. Undeterred, the preteen rehearsed even harder and returned to the stage two months later to show the world her growth as a dancer. "That's a Knowles right there," beamed her grandfather Mathew in the film. "Blue comes up fighting against the negativity that was put on her just because she was our kid," added her mother. "She was ready to take back her power."

Bey and Jay are each other's biggest fans—and sounding boards. Early in her solo career, she often brought the rapper into the studio to add lyrical finishing touches. As she evolved as an artist, the roles reversed. In 2017, Bey was instrumental in her husband's *4:44* album, a direct response to the infidelity-themed *Lemonade*. "Pillow talk is the strongest conversation on the planet. Every song has to get past her ears, in my eyes," Jay's producer No I.D. told the *New York Times*. "She came by a lot and played a good part in helping us get over hurdles on certain records." Her genius is indisputable, and when *Renaissance* was overlooked by the Grammys for Album of the Year in 2023, Jay defended his wife's musical masterpiece. "Look what it's done to the culture. Look how the energy of the world moved," he insisted in a 2023 *Tidal* interview. "When it just inspires creativity, that's an album. That has to be album of the year."

PART TWO

Making Musical Herstory

DISCOGRAPHY

Beyoncé is a certified hitmaker, with eighty-one singles over her three decades as a solo artist and as lead vocalist of Destiny's Child. And it's never the same old sound: each of her seven albums showcases her instinct for fusing R&B-pop with soul, funk, disco, rock, electronic, and gospel—as well as her evolution as a songwriter, from a young woman *Dangerously in Love* to mother-of-three having a *Renaissance*.

DANGEROUSLY IN LOVE

BEYONCÉ STEPS INTO THE SOLO SPOTLIGHT
RELEASE DATE: JUNE 23, 2003

• TRACK LIST •

1. Crazy in Love
   (featuring Jay-Z)

2. Naughty Girl

3. Baby Boy
   (featuring Sean Paul)

4. Hip Hop Star
   (featuring Big Boi and Sleepy Brown)

5. Be With You

6. Me, Myself and I

7. Yes

8. Signs
   (featuring Missy Elliott)

9. Speechless

10. That's How You Like It
    (featuring Jay-Z)

11. The Closer I Get to You
    (with Luther Vandross)

12. Dangerously in Love 2

13. Beyoncé Interlude

14. Gift from Virgo

15. Daddy

TRUE ROMANCE: As the title suggests, *Dangerously in Love* explores romance and its spectrum of emotions, from lust and obsession to insecurity and heartbreak. "There's something exciting when anything in life is a little scary, you know, and that's what I mean by dangerous," Bey told MTV News. "I don't mean you're going to hurt yourself or him." But who was she singing about? Ever since her 2002 collaboration with

Jay-Z on "'03 Bonnie & Clyde," rumors swirled the two were secretly dating. Confirming the relationship would have drummed up publicity for *Dangerously in Love*, but Bey chose to let her music do the talking. "I'm not trying to deny anything—or confirm anything," she teased the Associated Press. "Sometimes people lose touch with you being a human . . . I wanted people to know that I'm strong, but I can fall in love, I can get hurt, I can feel like I need someone, and everything every other woman goes through."

VERY DÉJÀ VU: *Dangerously in Love* sounded familiar to Destiny's Child fans—it's also the title of a song off the group's 2001 album, *Survivor*. The ballad's lyrics, cowritten by the singer, detail a romantic obsession, and as love was the theme of her solo effort, the track found new meaning. Bey re-recorded it with minor musical adjustments as "Dangerously in Love 2," which won a Grammy for Best Female R&B Vocal Performance in 2004 despite never being released as a single.

ARTISTIC LEAP: "I know that folks love me as a pop star," Beyoncé acknowledged to *Thread* magazine. "Now I want them to understand me as an artist." To introduce herself as a solo singer post-Destiny's Child, she reached deep into her musical roots, fusing R&B with hip-hop, soul, disco, and funk. As executive producer of *Dangerously in Love*, Bey personally selected her team of songwriters and producers, beginning with Scott Storch, then best known for his work with The Roots, Dr. Dre, Britney Spears, Justin Timberlake, Pink, and Christina Aguilera. In the studio, she whittled down the forty-three songs she recorded to fifteen and managed their mixing and mastering. "I was a little nervous about this album because I didn't think about selling records," Beyoncé admitted to the

New York Daily News. "I thought more about the artistry, growing as a writer and singer. I mean, I literally have a song without a chorus, with a Shuggie Otis sample" ("Gift from Virgo").

BROKEN RECORDS: Beyoncé became the first female artist to have the No. 1 album (*Dangerously in Love*) and the No. 1 single ("Crazy in Love") in the US and the UK at the same time. Only four male artists achieved the feat before her: the Beatles, Simon & Garfunkel, Rod Stewart, and Men at Work.

COVER STORY: The first look at Beyoncé as a solo artist had to be iconic—and she knew exactly what she wanted. Inspired by a Diamond.com campaign featuring French model Laetitia Casta sprawled across a bejeweled spiderweb, Bey contacted the ad's photographer, Markus Klinko, to bring her vision to life. For her glittering wardrobe, stylist (and mother) Tina Knowles asked jeweler Jose Barrera to redesign a pair of crystal leggings he had made for Cher in 1990 as a top for Beyoncé, "and the rest is history," Tina wrote on Instagram in 2021 to celebrate *Dangerously in Love*'s eighteenth anniversary. Today, the iconic fashion statement is on display at the Rock & Roll Hall of Fame in Cleveland, Ohio, alongside other Beyoncé relics including the titanium glove from her "Single Ladies" video and 2013 Super Bowl Halftime Show black leather-and-lace bodysuit.

CHART ATTACK: *Dangerously in Love* spawned five Top 10 singles, each showcasing a different dimension to Bey's talent and musical tastes. The first, "Crazy in Love" featuring then-rumored boyfriend Jay-Z, incorporates 1970s funk with R&B. Jamaican rapper Sean Paul lent his world-famous dancehall sound to the second single, "Baby Boy," which surpassed its predecessor to spend nine consecutive weeks at No. 1 on the *Billboard* Hot 100.

The singer wanted her third release to show depth, and "Me, Myself and I," about women listening to their inner voice, did just that as it burned up the charts for twenty-four weeks. Next, "Naughty Girl" (and its Studio 54–inspired music video) revealed her seductive side while also paying homage to Queen of Disco Donna Summers with a sample of her 1975 classic "Love to Love You Baby." Beyoncé honored another icon, Roberta Flack, for her debut's fifth and final single: a cover of "The Closer I Get to You," a duet with Luther Vandross that peaked at No. 2.

When Beyoncé presented the final cut to Columbia Records, "they told me I didn't have one single on my album," she revealed at a 2011 concert in New York City. "I guess they were kind of right. I had five."

LADIES FIRST: Following a ten-date Dangerously in Love Tour throughout Europe, Beyoncé joined Missy Elliott and Alicia Keys for a US trek in the spring of 2004. Billed as the "urban Lilith Fair," the Verizon Ladies First Tour made history as the first three-act show to feature several female R&B headliners. Beyoncé, whose five costume changes were custom designed by Dolce & Gabbana, emerged as the star of the show, which sold out New York's Madison Square Garden.

LASTING LEGACY: Two decades and six albums later, *Dangerously in Love* remains Beyoncé's best-selling album, with more than eleven million copies sold worldwide. At the 2004 *Grammys*, the debut won five of its six nominations—tying Bey with Lauryn Hill, Alicia Keys, and Norah Jones for the record of most Grammy Awards at a single ceremony.

B'DAY

HER 25TH BIRTHDAY GIFT TO FANS
RELEASE DATE: SEPTEMBER 4, 2006

• TRACK LIST •

1. Déjà Vu
   (featuring Jay-Z)

2. Get Me Bodied

3. Suga Mama

4. Upgrade U
   (featuring Jay-Z)

5. Ring the Alarm

6. Kitty Kat

7. Freakum Dress

8. Green Light

9. Irreplaceable

10. Resentment

11. Check On It
    (featuring Bun B. & Slim Thug)

12. Encore for the Fans

13. Listen
    (from the Motion Picture Soundtrack Dreamgirls*)*

GIRL (EM)POWER: Inspired by her *Dreamgirls* character, Deena, a singer controlled by her manager-husband, Beyoncé turned her second solo effort into a concept album about female empowerment that "speaks for every woman," she told *Billboard*. "I do things with my voice that I haven't done before." She also experimented with how she recorded the music, employing live instrumentation on several songs, most notably "Déjà Vu," which features bass guitar, hi-hat cymbals, and conga. Due to the emotional theme of the album—particularly, betrayal and infidelity—the songs naturally have an "aggressive" edge, Bey told MTV News. After portraying Deena for six months during the filming of the movie, "I had a lot to say. And the beats I was attracted to were a lot harder."

FAST TRACKS: After wrapping *Dreamgirls* in April 2006, Bey took off for a well-deserved month-long vacation—but her creative mind wouldn't relax. Without notifying her manager-father, Mathew Knowles, the singer quickly (and secretly) lined up a songwriting team and rented out Sony Music Studios in New York, where she installed four producers in separate rooms. For fourteen hours a day, Bey bounced between each, knocking out tracks with some of the best in the biz: Rodney "Darkchild" Jerkins, Swizz Beatz, Sean Garrett, and Rich Harrison. "I came to the studio and saw the zone. I said, 'Damn, everybody in here is banging out,'" Swizz Beatz recalled to MTV News. That friendly rivalry was precisely what Beyoncé had in mind. While working with Garrett, she strategically gushed about Harrison's "great beats," she told *Billboard*, with a laugh. "It was healthy competition." She recorded additional songs in Los Angeles with production duos Stargate ("Irreplaceable") and Pharrell Williams and Chad Hugo (aka the Neptunes) ("Green Light"). And just two weeks later, *B'Day* was completed.

CHART ATTACK: *B'Day* had a heyday: Beyoncé's second album spawned six singles. However, the commercial success of each was not a piece of birthday cake. "Déjà Vu" hit the Top 10 in eleven countries—yet fans were so disappointed in its music video's choreography, fashion, and editing, they started a petition for Bey to reshoot it. The second single "Ring the Alarm" was her highest debut at No. 12, but only climbed one spot to No. 11 before dropping off the charts. The third time was the charm: "Irreplaceable," with its catchy chorus, spent ten weeks at No. 1 and received a Grammy nomination for Record of the Year. Equally as successful was Bey's collaboration with Shakira, "Beautiful Liar," which appeared on the deluxe version of *B'Day* and peaked at No. 3. "Get Me Bodied" never made it past No. 68, and the final single, "Green Light," only performed well in the UK.

ROLE REVERSAL: "Irreplaceable," the biggest hit off the album, was cowritten with Ne-Yo, who penned the original lyrics from the male perspective—and as a country song, no less. On second thought, he realized it came off as "a little bit misogynistic" for a man to tell a woman she was replaceable, and the track soon found its way to Bey. She and Ne-Yo tailored the track for *B'Day* by revamping the musical and vocal arrangements, and the rest is history (or rather, *herstory*). In 2011, Ne-Yo revealed to Choice FM that he regretted giving away the chart-topper. "But that song actually taught me a very interesting lesson—men and women don't actually think that much differently on the grand scheme of things."

FALSE ALARM: Amid rumors that Jay-Z had cheated on Beyoncé with his protégé Rihanna, many speculated the other "chick on your arm" mentioned in "Ring the Alarm" hinted at the reported love triangle. Bey denied the claims, as did her father Mathew, who even put out a statement: "What will be next? Beyoncé's cut off all her hair? Dyed it green? Maybe she's singing the songs in reverse with some hidden subliminal message?"

VIDEO ALBUM: Six years before Beyoncé revolutionized the music industry with her self-titled visual album, she did a test run with *B'Day*

Anthology Video Album, a DVD of thirteen music videos released in conjunction with the album's 2007 deluxe edition. Each looks distinctly different, and all were creatively directed by the singer. "Some are in black and white. Some are Super8. Some are very bright, vivid colors. Some are, you know, they look a little retro," she told the Associated Press. "I wore my hair black in some. I wore '80s makeup in one of the videos. Sixties Mod makeup. It was so exciting 'cause I love fashion, I love dressing up, so definitely it was like playing different characters."

VIVA, BEYONCÉ: The singer embarked on a seven-month world tour in support of *B'Day*, The Beyoncé Experience, a Las Vegas–worthy spectacle of Bob Fosse–inspired dance numbers, disco balls, pyrotechnics, confetti, and glittering costumes designed by Giorgio Armani, Versace, Herve Leger, and Elie Saab.

DESTINY DELAYED: *B'Day* was originally slated for a 2004 release, imagined as a curated selection of B-sides that didn't make it onto *Dangerously in Love*. But her Destiny's Child duties called—the trio had to get back into the studio to record one last album, *Destiny Fulfilled*, which Beyoncé, Kelly, and Michelle promoted on their final tour, a five-month jaunt across four continents in 2005.

LATIN SURPRISE: About seven months after the release of *B'Day*, Beyoncé gifted her fans with the deluxe edition of the album. The album features ten more songs, including the chart-topping collaboration with Shakira, "Beautiful Liar," and Spanish versions of six of the original tracks.

BEAUTIFUL MUSIC

Beyoncé has been singing about cheaters since "Say My Name," but she put a new spin on the subject with "Beautiful Liar," a 2008 duet with Shakira told from each of their points of view after they realize they're dating the same guy. The song is a true partnership between Bey's R&B and the Colombian superstar's Latin-Arabic blend, as they trade lyrics revealing the untruths told to them by the "beautiful liar." By the chorus, they agree he's not worth their time. The song topped the charts in fifteen countries and earned a Grammy nomination for Best Pop Collaboration. At the 2007 *MTV Video Music Awards*, it won Most Earth-Shattering Collaboration—an understatement considering it has belly dancing, hip shaking, and an innovative sequence in which they mirror each other's movements. "I wanted us to play off the idea that we kind of look alike," Beyoncé told MTV News. "I saw this guy dancing once, and it looked like he was performing in the mirror until I realized [he was dancing with] another person, and I thought, 'How amazing!' So, we tried to do that."

I AM . . . SASHA FIERCE

BEY'S ALTER EGO SPEAKS UP
RELEASE DATE: NOVEMBER 12, 2008

• TRACK LIST •

I AM . . .

1. If I Were a Boy
2. Halo
3. Disappear
4. Broken-Hearted Girl
5. Ave Maria
6. Satellites

SASHA FIERCE

1. Single Ladies (Put a Ring on It)
2. Radio
3. Diva
4. Sweet Dreams
5. Video Phone

DOUBLE FEATURE: For her third album, Beyoncé introduced her bold alter-ego Sasha Fierce, while also staying true to her more reserved self: a double album, one for each persona. The six songs that comprise *I Am . . .* are more traditional R&B ballads "for my fans who've been there the whole time," she explained to *Billboard*. The Beyoncé they know and love, however, is actually more *Sasha Fierce*, whose sensual uptempo tracks reflect the "strong, fearless" stage persona she adopted early on in her career. "The double album allows me to take more risks and really step out of myself, or shall I say, step more into myself, and reveal a side of me that [only people who know me see]," Bey explained in a press release. "That's why half the record, *I Am . . .*, is about who I am underneath all the makeup, underneath the lights, and underneath all the exciting star drama."

THE WRITE STUFF: As a teenager, Beyoncé wrote some of the biggest hits on the planet with Destiny's Child—and the twenty-six-year-old hoped to showcase her creative evolution on her third solo album. Heading into the studio for *I Am . . . Sasha Fierce*, "I knew that, artistically, I had to grow," she revealed in a press release. "I feel like at this point, I wanted people to hear songs with stronger lyrics and songs that made you feel . . . Lyrically, it's the best album I've ever had. If a song didn't say anything or mean anything to me, I didn't put it on the record."

SMOOTH SOUNDS: Interestingly, for the *I Am . . .* tracks, Beyoncé experimented with genres not previously known to her, particularly folk, alternative rock, and adult contemporary. "Some of it sounds like Barbra Streisand, Karen Carpenter, and the Beatles around the 1970s," she explained to *Billboard*. To achieve that, she worked with a new team of producers, including Babyface, OneRepublic's Ryan Tedder, The-Dream, and Tricky Stewart.

Bey also collaborated with songwriter Amanda Ghost, who penned "Beautiful Liar" for *B'Day*. On *I Am . . .*, the pair retooled the lyrics of Franz Schubert's 1825 composition "Ave Maria," which Bey performed at her wedding earlier that year. This modern version very much reflected the superstar's life, Ghost explained to the *Daily Telegraph*. "She talks about being surrounded by friends but she's alone," and then how it's only the two of them when the lights go out. "I think that's probably the most personal line on the whole album about her and Jay, because they are very real, and they're very much in love, and it must be pretty tough to have that love when you're incredibly famous."

SINGLES LADY: Because *I Am . . . Sasha Fierce* is a double album, lead singles were released from each respective collection: "If I Were a Boy," which peaked at No. 3 on the *Billboard* Hot 100 chart, and the No. 1 smash hit "Single Ladies (Put a Ring on It)." By this time, Jay-Z already had—he and Bey said "I do" six months earlier. But for Sasha Fierce, it was an anthem for empowering those dealing with commitment issues. "In my life, when I put on the stilettos, it's all about being confident, sometimes overly confident, and hearing all the things that women need to hear to boost themselves and go out and to move on," Beyoncé explained in a press release.

For the second set of singles, Bey put out hip-hop "Diva" and "Halo," with the angelic power ballad topping charts all over the world. Over the years, she has performed the moving track during times of significant tragedy: Michael Jackson's death in 2009, the 2010 Haiti earthquake that claimed the lives of an estimated 160,000 people, and the 2020 memorial for Kobe Bryant and his thirteen-year-old daughter, Gianna, who both perished in a helicopter crash.

Five other singles were released off *I Am . . . Sasha Fierce*, although none moved the needle quite like "Single Ladies" or "Halo."

FINAL REQUEST: MTV's video countdown show, *Total Request Live*, was instrumental in launching Beyoncé's career, first with Destiny's Child and then as a solo artist. So it only made sense for the superstar to take part in its final episode on November 16, 2008, and close out the iconic program with a three-song medley—"If I Were a Boy," "Single Ladies," and "Crazy in Love"—live from New York's Times Square.

COVER STORY: The double album had two covers: one for each persona. Both images are arresting—intimate closeups of Beyoncé, shot in black and white. But if it had been up to the record label, *I Am . . . Sasha Fierce* would have been in color. Bey put her foot down, she revealed in a 2021 interview for *Harper's Bazaar*. "They told me I wouldn't sell if it wasn't in color. That was ridiculous . . . Who did they ask?" The superstar was so insulted, she doubled down on her third album's artistic angle. "I was so exhausted and annoyed with these formulaic corporate companies that I based my whole next project off of black and white photography, including the videos for 'Single Ladies' and 'If I Were a Boy' and all of the artwork by Peter Lindbergh for *I Am . . . Sasha Fierce*, which ended up being my biggest commercial success to date. I try to keep the human feeling and spirit and emotion in my decision-making."

BROKEN RECORDS: At the 2009 *Grammys*, Beyoncé was recognized for *I Am . . . Sasha Fierce*, winning six awards including Album of the Year—the most wins in one night by a female artist.

REST IN PEACE: After the *I Am . . . Sasha Fierce* cycle, she got back to *I Am . . . Beyoncé*. In 2010, the singer announced to *Allure* magazine that "Sasha Fierce is done. I killed her" (figuratively speaking, of course). But why drop the popular alter ego? "Because I've grown and now I'm able to merge the two."

4

• TRACK LIST •

1. 1+1
2. I Care
3. I Miss You
4. Best Thing I Never Had
5. Party
   (featuring Andre 3000)
6. Rather Die Young

7. Start Over
8. Love on Top
9. Countdown
10. End of Time
11. I Was Here
12. Run the World (Girls)

INSPIRATION EVERYWHERE: After the grueling I Am . . . World Tour, an "overwhelmed and overworked" Beyoncé took some much-needed time off from the spotlight. For an entire year, she traveled the world, read books, watched films, ate whatever she wanted, went to concerts with friends, even rode a toboggan down the Great Wall of China. "I was in such a great peaceful state, it inspired purity," she revealed in the 2011 MTV special *Beyoncé: Year of 4.*

LUCKY NUMBER: 4 is Bey's fourth album, and also her favorite number: her birthday is September 4, Jay-Z's is December 4, and they were married on April 4 (4/4). It's that connection that also inspired their daughter Blue's middle name, Ivy, the phonetic spelling of IV, the Roman numeral for four. All the same, *4* was not Bey's original title for her album. "Everywhere I look, I see [fans] calling it *4*," she told *Billboard* ahead of its release. "I had a whole other name and concept, but I keep seeing that the fans love the name *4*, and I think it would be a really nice thing to let them name the record."

SOLO STAR: After two decades of being managed by her father, Beyoncé ended their working relationship in 2010. "A real change meant separating from him," she admitted in *Year of 4*. "It was scary, but it empowered me, and I wasn't going to let fear stop me." Not only did Bey evolve, but so did her artistry on her fourth album. "It's bolder than the music on my previous albums because I'm bolder," she wrote on her website. "The more mature I become and the more life experiences I have, the more I have to talk about. I really focused on songs being classics, songs that would last, songs that I could sing when I'm forty and when I'm sixty."

MUSIC & LYRICS: After experimenting on her previous album, Bey brought it back to the basics for *4*: traditional R&B with soul-rock grooves. Displeased with the lack of variety in contemporary music, she took on the challenge of "figuring out a way to get R&B back on the radio," she told *Complex*. "Everything sounds the same on the radio. With *4* I tried to mix R&B from the '70s and the '90s with rock 'n' roll and a lot of horns to create something new and exciting. I wanted musical changes, bridges, vibrata, live instrumentation, and classic songwriting."

The emotions of the professional split from her father ignited her most personal lyrics to date, particularly centered around the theme of female empowerment, like lead single "Run the World (Girls)." "I try to write songs and sing songs that we as women need to hear," she said on ABC's *Good Morning America*. "I know sometimes it's hard to realize how amazing we are. I'm very happy to be able to do that to women around the world."

THE ONE: With more than seventy songs written and recorded, it was an overwhelming task to edit the sheer volume of work. After whittling it down to twenty-two, Bey crowd-sourced the final tracklist. In a clip from *Year of 4*, she gathers her team and hands each person a piece of paper with instructions to rank their top ten choices. When the votes are tallied, everyone's favorite song is "Countdown," a 1990s-esque ode to Jay-Z with a catchy chorus.

NEW TALENT: The singer added several collaborators to her team for *4*, from established artists Kanye West and Andre 3000 on the 1980s-sounding "Party" to newcomer Frank Ocean, who wrote the ballad "I Miss You" at Queen Bey's request after she heard his *Nostalgia, Ultra* mixtape. "Jay had a CD playing in the car one Sunday when we were driving to Brooklyn," she recalled to *Complex*. "I noticed his tone, his arrangements, and his storytelling. I immediately reached out to him—literally the next morning. I asked him to fly to New York and work on my record."

COVER STORY: After the stark look of *I Am . . . Sasha Fierce*, Beyoncé went super glam for *4*. The cover image illustrates the theme of the album, with the singer striking a powerful pose in a fox-fur stole by Alexandre Vauthier embellished with Swarovski crystals from atop the roof of Le Meurice hotel in Paris. Similarly for the deluxe edition of 4, she rocks a purple-and-black beaded dress by Maxime Simoens. The French designers were two of the up-and-coming creators enlisted by Bey's stylist Ty Hunter and creative director Jenke Ahmed Tailly.

FIRST LADY: Just two days after dropping 4, Beyoncé became the first solo female artist in twenty years to headline the Pyramid Stage at the Glastonbury Festival in Somerset, England. An honor typically reserved for rock bands, the announcement was not well-received—but Bey would prove the skeptics wrong. Bey called on her talented friends Coldplay's Chris Martin and U2's Bono to help with the setlist: twenty-five songs spanning her career, including 4's "Best Thing I Never Had," "End of Time," "1+1," and "Run the World (Girls)," plus covers of Kings of Leon's "Sex on Fire" and Prince's "The Beautiful Ones."

When Bey took the stage for Glastonbury's final night, she had the world in the palm of her hand for ninety minutes. With a record-breaking 2.6 million people watching in the UK—and a portion of her set airing simultaneously on BET in the US—the American singer delivered a career-defining performance heralded by fans and critics alike. "I've done a lot of things in my life, but I have never performed in front of 175,000 people," Bey told the crowd, which included her husband, Jay-Z, mother, Tina, and friend Gwyneth Paltrow. Looking back on the night with the BBC, she gushed there was "so much love and unity in the audience. It was beautiful."

MRS. CARTER TOUR

Beyoncé took her first four albums on the road with The Mrs. Carter World Tour, her biggest production to date with 132 concerts across North America, South America, Europe, and Oceania. As the reigning Queen Bey, her show had a royal theme inspired by Marie Antoinette, Elizabeth I, and Cleopatra. For the tour art, Bey channeled the eighteenth-century French monarch in a vintage Thierry Mugler gold corset accessorized with a jeweled scepter and a crown. A promotional video expands on the majesty, as ladies-in-waiting dress Bey for a dance that's deejayed by a court jester. The twenty-song setlist opened with "Run the World (Girls)" and ran through four albums of hits with a medley of "Halo" and Whitney Houston's "I Will Always Love You" as the encore. Eight months into the tour, she dropped the surprise album *Beyoncé* and integrated several tracks, such as "Drunk in Love" and "XO," for the remainder of the run. The Mrs. Carter World Tour grossed $229.7 million, the most for any solo artist in 2013.

BEYONCÉ

SELF-TITLED SURPRISE ALBUM
RELEASE DATE: DECEMBER 13, 2013

• TRACK LIST •

1. Pretty Hurts

2. Haunted

3. Drunk in Love
   (featuring Jay-Z)

4. Blow

5. No Angel

6. Partition

7. Jealous

8. Rocket

9. Mine
   (featuring Drake)

10. XO

11. ***Flawless
    (featuring Chimamanda Ngozi Adichie)

12. Superpower
    (featuring Frank Ocean)

13. Heaven

14. Blue
    (featuring Blue Ivy)

PLATINUM EDITION

15. 7/11

16. Flawless Remix
    (featuring Nicki Minaj)

17. Drunk in Love (Remix)
    (featuring Jay-Z & Kanye West)

18. Ring Off

19. Blow Remix
    (featuring Pharrell Williams)

20. Standing on the Sun Remix
    (featuring Mr. Vegas)

DOUBLE SHOCKER: "Surprise!" That's all Beyoncé wrote on Instagram to caption a mysterious video montage that flashed "visual album" and "available now." Fans who were still awake (after all, it was midnight on the East Coast) rushed to the iTunes Store to find *Beyoncé*: a self-titled collection of new songs, plus a music video for each—making it the first-ever visual album.

How did she keep it all a secret from the world? A small circle of trust. Although it was widely assumed Bey was working on her next album, no one knew the specific timeline, not even her label, Columbia Records. In early December 2013, her management company, Parkwood Entertainment, met with Columbia executives and select iTunes representatives to discuss "*Lily*," a code name for the album they used to prevent the news from leaking. To further throw fans off the scent, Columbia chairman Rob Stringer announced some of the label's major releases slated for 2014, with Beyoncé's expected "at some point" that year. Instead, four days later her self-titled sensation dropped on iTunes, which held the exclusive for seven days as physical copies of the album were manufactured for retailers.

IMMERSIVE EXPERIENCE: "I see music. It's more than just what I hear," Bey explained in the *Self-Titled: Part 1* documentary. "When I'm connected to something, I immediately see a visual or a series of images that are tied to a feeling or an emotion, a memory from my childhood, thoughts about life, my dreams or my fantasies—and they're all connected to the music . . . I wanted people to hear the songs with the story that's in my head because it's what makes it mine. That vision in my brain is what I wanted people to experience the first time." Inspired by Michael Jackson's iconic "Thriller" video, which debuted on MTV in 1983, Beyoncé set out to recreate her own immersive experience, especially for fans living in the new era of streaming music, where it's much easier to skip ahead after a few seconds of a song instead of investing in the intended artistry.

CAMP BEYONCÉ: After giving birth to her first daughter, Blue Ivy, in January 2012, the singer didn't take much of a maternity leave; she began recording her fifth album that summer. But instead of spending long hours in the studio, Beyoncé brought the studio to her: She invited her songwriting team, which included Justin Timberlake, Sia, Timbaland, and The-Dream, to move into her Hamptons home for a month. "We had dinners with the producers every day, like a family," Bey told *Vogue*. "It was like a camp. Weekends off. You could go and jump in the pool and ride bikes . . . the ocean and grass and sunshine . . . It was really a safe place."

FLAWS AND ALL: Described as an album of "anti-perfection," *Beyoncé* finds beauty in flaws. That's explored on "***Flawless," which includes audio of her 1993 *Star Search* loss (a defining moment for the young singer), and "Pretty Hurts," a ballad about society's impossibly high standards. "The amount of personal growth from this project isn't like anything I've ever done," she admitted to fans during a Beyoncé event in New York. "I took all of my insecurities, all of my doubts, all of my fears and everything I've learned over the seventeen years, and I applied it into this project."

The imperfect theme also carried over to the visual album's content. Several videos were shot with little to no preparation and came together on location. "There's something about that freedom that is different for me," Bey admitted in *Self-Titled: Part 3*. "I'm trying to rebel against perfection. It's fun because you never know what could happen." She put all her faith in director Terry Richardson's vision for "XO," filmed at Coney Island in Brooklyn. While filming a scene set inside an arcade, he suggested opening the door and walking into a crowd of hundreds gathered outside. Beyoncé agreed, and what Richardson captured was a raw and rare moment between the superstar and her fans. "We went with feeling, we went with instinct," described Richardson. "It's a beautiful cycle of energy."

SHE IS MOTHER: The first collection of music Bey released since giving birth, it was important to show the world that becoming "a mother doesn't mean you lose who you are," Bey revealed in *Self-Titled: Part 4.* And in the process, she rediscovered her old self. "Recording this album was such an outlet for me to kind of escape and create whatever world and fantasy definitely at the time was not happening." The moment she heard the beat for "Partition," something about it took her back to the early days of her romance with Jay-Z when he thought of her as "the hottest thing in the world." As she imagined an X-rated hookup in the backseat of their chauffeured car, she hopped on the microphone to freestyle the lyrics and hit record.

Bey's "Partition" fantasy came to life for its video. Shot at Crazy Horse cabaret club in Paris—the same place she and Jay-Z celebrated their engagement—she wanted to recreate "the ultimate sexy show" for her husband. As he watches from the audience, Bey writhes around the stage in next to nothing. After dropping sixty-five pounds (29 kg) of baby weight, "I wanted to show my body," she said in *Part 3.* "I wanted to show that you can have a child and you can work hard and you can get your body back. I'm still finding my sensuality, getting back into my body, being proud of growing up. It was important that I expressed that in this music."

COVER STORY: Of all Beyoncé's albums, her self-titled collection is the only one to not feature the superstar on the cover. Creative director Todd

Tourso felt so "inundated with imagery" from the tracklist's seventeen visuals, he decided to just keep it simple: "Beyoncé" spelled out in a typeface derived from boxing-ring placards "that is kind of masculine but still sexy and loud," he explained to *The Atlantic*. The inspiration? The cover of Metallica's 1991 self-titled album, which is all black with the band's logo in one corner and a coiled snake in the other. For *Beyoncé*, Tourso went with a grayed-out pink font color, a "subversion of femininity," while the smaller size of the centered logo reflects "this idea of almost being naked and stripped down, but also confident."

BROKEN RECORDS: Despite having no advanced single or marketing campaign, the surprise album debuted at No. 1, selling nearly 1 million copies worldwide in three days—making it the fastest-selling album in the history of the iTunes Store at the time. At the 2015 *Grammys*, *Beyoncé* was nominated for five awards and won three, including Best R&B Song for "Drunk in Love."

TEN YEARS LATER: On December 13, 2023, the singer dropped another surprise video on Instagram, this time in honor of *Beyoncé*'s tenth anniversary. Using much of the same footage from her original announcement, the celebratory clip also includes a throwback fan reaction—plus a soundbite from Bey's 2014 collaboration with Nicki Minaj, "Feeling Myself," that sums up her historic success.

SELF-TITLED REFLECTION

On the one-year anniversary of *Beyoncé*, the singer celebrated its record-breaking success with a gift for her fans: *Yours and Mine*, a cinematic retrospective that combines footage from her self-titled album's visuals with abstract imagery as she muses about fame, feminism, and family. "I sometimes wish I could just be anonymous and walk down the street just like everyone else," she admits in the twelve-minute short film, a vulnerable glimpse at her internal struggles. "Now that I'm famous it's really, really difficult to do very simple things." Luckily for Bey, she has someone who understands exactly how she feels: her husband, Jay-Z. "And when you find the person that you trust and you love and you feel is going to respect you and take all the shit that you have and turn it around and bring out the best in you, it feeds you. It is the most powerful thing you can ever feel in your life."

LEMONADE

WHEN LIFE GAVE HER LEMONS . . .

RELEASE DATE: APRIL 23, 2016

• TRACK LIST •

1. Pray You Catch Me

2. Hold Up

3. Don't Hurt Yourself
   (featuring Jack White)

4. Sorry

5. 6 Inch
   (featuring the Weeknd)

6. Daddy Lessons

7. Love Drought

8. Sandcastles

9. Forward
   (featuring James Blake)

10. Freedom
    (featuring Kendrick Lamar)

11. All Night

12. Formation

DELUXE EDITION

13. Sorry (Original Demo)

SOUR NOTE: A concept album about her husband's infidelity, *Lemonade* follows Beyoncé's healing journey over eleven stages—from "Intuition" to "Redemption"—with each correlating to a specific song (excluding Track 12, "Formation"). During the creative process, she associated her pain with the "generational curses" of her ancestors: "broken male-female relationships, abuse of power, and mistrust," she revealed to *Vogue*. "Only when I saw that clearly was I able to resolve those conflicts in my own relationship. Connecting to the past and knowing our history makes us both bruised and beautiful." One trauma she knew firsthand was her father's extramarital relationship, which she works through in "Daddy Lessons," *Lemonade*'s Accountability chapter.

As for the album's title, Beyoncé borrowed it from her husband's grandmother, Hattie White, who told those gathered at her ninetieth birthday party, "I had my ups and downs, but I always find the inner strength to pull myself up. I was served lemons, but I made lemonade." To represent her own family, Bey included her maternal grandmother's lemonade recipe, passed down over generations, in the album's artwork.

MUSICAL MEDLEY: Bey continued to evolve her sound with *Lemonade*, experimenting with rock ("Don't Hurt Yourself") and country ("Daddy Issues"). And she worked with some of the best in their respective genres. White Stripes frontman Jack White co-wrote, co-produced, and is featured on "Don't Hurt Yourself," which earned a Grammy nomination for Best Rock Performance.

"Daddy Issues," Bey's first-ever attempt at country music, was criticized for being a loose interpretation of the genre—and even rejected by the Recording Academy's country music committee. So for the remix, she brought on bonafide country stars (and fellow Texans) the Chicks. The Dallas-based trio joined Houston's brightest star for a performance of "Daddy Issues" at the 2016 *Country Music Association Awards*, which went on to win Collaboration of the Year at the 2017 *CMAs*.

VISIBLE PAIN: Expanding on the precedent she set with *Beyoncé*, the singer created a sixty-five-minute visual accompaniment for *Lemonade*—a musical film featuring Blue Ivy, Serena Williams, Zendaya, Chloe x Halle, Amandla Stenberg, and Academy Award–nominated actress Quvenzhané

Wallis, as well as the mothers of murdered Black men Trayvon Martin, Michael Brown, and Eric Garner. Described by *Billboard* as "a revolutionary work of Black feminism," *Lemonade* depicts the historical impact of slavery on Black love. "My intention for the film and album was to create a body of work that would give a voice to our pain, our struggles, our darkness and our history," Beyoncé explained at the 2017 *Grammys*. "It's important to me to show images to my children that reflect their beauty, so they can grow up in a world where they look in the mirror . . . and see themselves, and have no doubt that they're beautiful, intelligent, and capable."

BREAKING RECORDS: *Lemonade* was Bey's sixth consecutive album to debut at No. 1 on the *Billboard* Hot 200 (beginning with her first release), surpassing the record previously held by rapper DMX. In 2022, she outdid herself when *Renaissance* also entered the charts at the top spot.

POWERFUL MESSAGE: *Lemonade*'s first single, "Formation," is a feminist anthem that honors Black heritage and culture. The video goes even deeper, showing the historical impact of slavery, racism, and police brutality. Set in New Orleans in the aftermath of Hurricane Katrina, which especially devastated Black communities, "Formation" opens with Beyoncé standing on the roof of a police car submerged in water, sinking further as the video progresses (and ultimately enveloped by the rising tide). "Formation" was named Best Music Video of the year by the *Grammys* and MTV and praised by *Rolling Stone* as being the greatest video of all time.

OMG, BECKY: The fourth track, "Sorry," follows Bey unapologetically coping with a cheater. By the end, she's ready to move on, telling the guy in question to find someone named Becky. Who? Fans speculated "Becky" could be anyone from the couple's longtime friend Gwyneth Paltrow to singer Rita Ora. Fashion designer Rachel Roy threw herself into the mix with an Instagram photo captioned, "Good hair don't care, but we will take good lighting, for selfies, or self-truths always," which the BeyHive interpreted as an admission of guilt—and they swarmed. Roy subsequently deleted the post and released a statement insisting she was not Becky: "There is no validity to the idea that the song references me personally."

WORLD FORMATION: Named after *Lemonade*'s lead single, the Formation World Tour was Beyoncé's first solo all-stadium tour. And it was quite a spectacle, with a sixty-foot (18 m) LED centerpiece dubbed The Monolith that rotated for each act of the show and a second stage filled with two thousand gallons (7,571 L) of water. Kicking off just four days after *Lemonade*'s release, the tour made its sold-out trek across North America and Europe, grossing $256 million in 2016.

JAY-Z REACTS: As Beyoncé processed her emotions in the studio, her husband did the same—in the next room, no less. But it would be another year before Jay-Z released his answer to *Lemonade*, *4:44*, the exact time he awoke one night to write the title track. Proving that all was forgiven between the couple, Beyoncé made an appearance on the musical mea culpa, lending her voice to "Family Feud" and appearing in its video (along with daughter Blue Ivy). Jay-Z also did his own work to save his marriage from divorce, he revealed to the *New York Times*. "The hardest thing is seeing pain on someone's face that you caused, and then have to deal with yourself."

LION QUEENS

Five years after starring in the remake of *The Lion King*, Beyoncé returned to the Disney-animated franchise for the 2024 prequel, *Mufasa: The Lion King*—and she brought along one of her own cubs. Blue Ivy voices Kiara, the daughter of Bey's Queen Nala and King Simba (Donald Glover). The plot tells the tale of how her grandfather, Mufasa (Aaron Pierre), became the greatest king of the Pride Lands, told to Kiara by Rafiki (John Kane) through flashbacks. The *Mufasa* director, Barry Jenkins, came up with the idea to cast Blue after hearing her narration in the audiobook of *Hair Love*, a 2019 children's book about learning to love one's natural hair. "The quality of her voice, I just thought it felt like this character," he told *People*. Jenkins sees *Mufasa* as "kind of like this snapshot, this time capsule of a moment in their lives that I think is really beautiful." Production began in 2021, two years before Blue joined the Renaissance World Tour as a featured dancer.

RENAISSANCE

BEYONCÉ ENTERS HER GREATEST ERA
RELEASE DATE: JULY 29, 2022

• TRACK LIST •

1. I'M THAT GIRL
2. COZY
3. ALIEN SUPERSTAR
4. CUFF IT
5. ENERGY
(featuring Beam)
6. BREAK MY SOUL
7. CHURCH GIRL
8. PLASTIC OFF THE SOFA

9. VIRGO'S GROOVE
10. MOVE
(featuring Grace Jones and Tems)
11. HEATED
12. THIQUE
13. ALL UP IN YOUR MIND
14. AMERICA HAS A PROBLEM
15. PURE/HONEY
16. SUMMER RENAISSANCE

ESCAPE ARTIST: Just like billions of people all over the world, Beyoncé spent the better part of 2020 in lockdown due to the coronavirus pandemic. And just like it did to many people, the global pandemic forced her to re-evaluate. The introspection unlocked a whole new level of her artistry. "Creating this album allowed me a place to dream and to find escape during a scary time for the world," Beyoncé explained in the *Renaissance* press release. "It allowed me to feel free and adventurous in a time when little else was moving . . . It was a beautiful journey of exploration."

CLUB RENAISSANCE: As fans emerged from that dark place, Beyoncé lit the way with her first album in six years, a collection of dance music heavily inspired by the 1970s. It wasn't just the era's sound Bey was going for, but its vibe at a time when marginalized visionaries, specifically Black and queer musicians, produced art without constraint. Coming into her own *Renaissance*, the singer put a fresh modern spin on retro genres, mixing disco and house with funk, techno, hip-hop, and dancehall for a sixteen-track collection that plays like a DJ mix with seamless beat-matching transitions between songs.

WATCH THE THRONE: As the BeyHive buzzed over *Renaissance*, the Queen made it a point to share her crown with those who inspired her: "Thank you to all of the pioneers who originate culture, to all of the fallen angels whose contributions have gone unrecognized for far too long," she wrote on Instagram. "This is a celebration for you." However, for several creators, it was also a celebration *with* them.

Bey samples legendary underground drag queens Kevin Aviance and Moi Renee on "Pure/Honey," a total shock to Aviance when *Renaissance* dropped and his phone started ringing off the hook. Ts Madison, a Black transgender woman, is also highlighted on "Cozy," which features audio from a 2020 viral video she made in reaction to the deaths of Iyanna Dior, also a trans woman, and George Floyd days apart in Minneapolis. The global exposure from Beyoncé elevated the message, Madison explained to *Essence*: "She said let it be known that we are all Black in totality."

Going back even further into the pop culture history books, the lead single, "Break My Soul," borrows the hook of 1993's "Show Me Love" by Robin S, a house-music hitmaker whose last album came out a year before Destiny's Child's debut. "Thank you so much for giving me my flowers while I'm still alive," the singer joked on *Good Morning Britain*. "I am honored, and I'm excited to see what else can happen." Living legend Grace Jones also lent her unmistakable voice to "Move," a rarity for the Studio 54 nightclub fixture. "I'm a born-alone, die-alone, sing-alone kind of girl," she explained to *Vogue*. But after meeting the superstar, Jones reconsidered. "She was very, very sweet, so I said okay."

COVER STORY: Beyoncé became a work of art for *Renaissance*: the singer, wearing a chrome rhinestone body harness, sits astride a holographic crystal horse. Although she's never publicly commented on the cover image, shot by Dutch photographer Carlijn Jacobs, fans have their theories. Given Bey's waist-length hair, some think it's an allusion to Lady Godiva, the eleventh-century English noblewoman who protested unjust taxation by riding a horse through the streets while nude. Others note *Renaissance*'s disco theme as evidence that the cover is actually a nod to Bianca Jagger, who was famously photographed on a horse at Studio 54 in 1977.

HINT, HINT: In celebration of turning forty, Bey looked back at her extraordinary life in a 2021 essay for *Harper's Bazaar*. Turning her focus toward the future, she revealed her hope—and dropped a major Easter egg about her next album. "I feel a renaissance emerging, and I want to be part of nurturing that escape in any way possible," she teased.

HEARD, NOT SEEN: After back-to-back visual albums, the same was expected for *Renaissance*—but fans would have to make their own lemonade out of the disappointing news that Beyoncé "decided to lead without visuals." According to the official press release: "It is a chance again to be listeners and not viewers, while taking in every gem of the pristine production." A week later, fans again got their hopes up when Bey dropped an "official teaser" for "I'm That Girl," featuring a quick montage of the singer in twenty different looks before the screen fades to black. However, that was the one and only glimpse at a *Renaissance* visual. On tour in 2023, concertgoers went as far as holding up signs asking for an update. "You are the visuals, baby," Beyoncé told one fan in Louisville, Kentucky.

SIMPLY HER BEST: Beyoncé's most innovative material to date, *Renaissance* was ranked the best album of 2022 by music critics from two dozen publications including *Rolling Stone*, the *New York Times*, the *Los Angeles Times*, *Entertainment Weekly*, Pitchfork, *The Hollywood Reporter*, and NPR.

HOLY TRINITY: Announced in 2022 as a "three-act project," Bey's seventh album is officially titled *Act I: Renaissance*, with 2024's *Cowboy Carter* as *Act II*. What can fans expect from the final part of the trilogy? Only the Queen knows for sure—but that hasn't silenced speculation. Among the genres fans think she might explore in *Act III* are rock, opera, and jazz.

COWBOY CARTER

BEYONCÉ GETS A LITTLE BIT COUNTRY
RELEASE DATE: MARCH 29, 2024

• TRACK LIST •

1. American Requiem

2. Blackbiird
   (with Brittney Spencer, Reyna Roberts, Tanner Adell, and Tiera Kennedy)

3. 16 Carriages

4. Protector
   (with Rumi Carter)

5. My Rose

6. Smoke Hour / Willie Nelson
   (with Willie Nelson)

7. Texas Hold 'Em

8. Bodyguard

9. Dolly P
   (with Dolly Parton)

10. Jolene

11. Daughter

12. Spaghettii
    (with Linda Martell and Shaboozey)

13. Alligator Tears

14. Smoke Hour II
    (with Willie Nelson)

15. Just For Fun
    (with Willie Jones)

16. II Most Wanted
    (with Miley Cyrus)

17. Levii's Jeans
    (with Post Malone)

18. Flamenco

19. The Linda Martell Show
    (with Linda Martell)

20. Ya Ya

21. Oh Louisiana

22. Desert Eagle

23. Riiverdance

24. II Hands II Heaven

25. Tyrant
    (with Dolly Parton)

26. Sweet / Honey / Buckiin'
    (with Shaboozey)

27. Amen

URBAN COWGIRL: Nearly a decade in the making, *Cowboy Carter* is Beyoncé's response to the backlash she faced at the 2016 *Country Music Association (CMA) Awards*, when she performed *Lemonade*'s "Daddy Lessons" with the Chicks. According to detractors, she didn't belong in the genre and the CMA even deleted all promotional content related to Bey's appearance—even though it helped boost the show's ratings to the highest of its fifty-year history.

She began writing the album in 2019 and recorded over a hundred songs during the pandemic, with the intention of releasing *Cowboy Carter* before *Renaissance*, but at the time "there was too much heaviness in the world," Beyoncé said in a statement. "We wanted to dance. We deserved to dance. But I had to trust God's timing." By swapping the two albums, she gave herself more time to explore the history of country music and its discrimination against Black artists.

Bey announced "new music" in a Verizon commercial that aired during the Super Bowl. Immediately following, a video posted on her Instagram account teased *Act II* with a snippet of "Texas Hold 'Em," one of two songs she dropped at midnight alongside the ballad "16 Carriages."

RADIO BEYONCÉ: Whereas *Renaissance*'s track list played like a seamless DJ club mix, the concept of *Cowboy Carter* is a fictional radio station, KNTRY Radio Texas, hosted by an all-star lineup of country music pioneers: Dolly Parton, Willie Nelson, and Linda Martell. In the interlude, "Dolly P," the reigning Queen of Country, introduces Queen Bey's reimagining of her 1973 hit "Jolene," which references *Lemonade*'s Becky as the other woman this time. Marijuana legalization activist Nelson hosts the appropriately titled "Smoke Hour," a twenty-second snippet that leads into "Texas Hold 'Em."

Martell, the first Black female singer to perform at the Grand Ole Opry, is featured in spoken-word segments at the beginning of "Spaghettii" and in her own interlude, "The Linda Martell Show." Exposure on *Cowboy Carter* introduced the South Carolina native to a whole new generation, and streams of Martell's music surged 127,430 percent.

SADDLE UP: From disco queen to rodeo queen! Just like *Act I, Renaissance*, Beyoncé sits atop a horse (this one real, not holographic) for the cover of *Act II, Cowboy Carter*. Also like in its predecessor, her hair (now blonde) is several feet long and whipping in the wind to illustrate the horse's speed. The portrait, shot by Texas native Blair Caldwell, shows the singer riding sidesaddle, holding the reins in one hand and an American flag in the other. As for the album's title, "the word cowboy itself was used in a derogatory way to describe the former slaves as 'boys,' who were the most skilled and had the hardest jobs of handling horses and cattle, alike," Beyoncé explained in a press release. "In destroying the negative connotation, what remains is the strength and resiliency of these men who were the true definition of Western fortitude."

WANTED WOMEN: Beyoncé collaborates with Dolly's goddaughter, Miley Cyrus, on "II Most Wanted," the album's third single, which debuted at No. 2 on the Hot Country Songs chart. The country-pop track features an interpolation of Fleetwood Mac's "Landslide" and follows a ride-or-die relationship à la *Thelma and Louise*. "I've loved Beyoncé since long before I had the opportunity to meet and work with her," Miley gushed on social media. "My admiration runs so much deeper now that I've created alongside of her. Thank you Beyoncé. You're everything and more."

COWBOY KNOWLES

Born and raised in Texas, Beyoncé is no stranger to the country scene. As a kid, she regularly attended the local Houston Livestock Show and Rodeo, considered the largest of its kind in the world with an average attendance of 2.5 million. As a superstar, she's returned to her old stomping ground to perform at the annual event four times between 2001 and 2007. Over the years, the "amazing diverse and multicultural experience" stayed with her.

In 2021, Bey reimagined her childhood memories with Ivy Park's Rodeo collection—apparel and accessories that fused classic streetwear with the Black cowboy experience. Musically, she was also strongly influenced by childhood experiences. Bey spent every summer with her paternal family three states away in Alabama, and it was there that she received an education in country music from her grandfather. "He used to sing to her," Mathew Knowles told the BBC in 2024. "At an early age, she heard this music. And when you're two, three years old, subconsciously music stays in your head."

GENERATIONAL TALENTS: Track 2 is a cover of the Beatles' "Blackbird" (stylized as "Blackbiird" in reference to *Act II*) backed by a chorus of up-and-coming Black country artists: Brittney Spencer, Reyna Roberts, Tanner Adell, and Tiera Kennedy. The inclusion of minority women trying to make it in a primarily white genre is a poignant nod at the song's lyrical inspiration. In 1968, at the end of the Civil Rights era, Paul McCartney was appalled by footage of the Little Rock Nine—Black teenagers who required military protection at a formerly all-white high school following its desegregation. The Beatles singer-songwriter gave Bey his blessing to remake the classic and carry on its message five decades later. "I can't believe that still in these days there are places where this kind of thing is happening right now," McCartney wrote on Instagram. "Anything my song and Beyoncé's fabulous version can do to ease racial tension would be a great thing and makes me very proud."

Adell, whose voice is also featured on "American Requiem," conjured her career-defining collaboration after Beyoncé announced *Cowboy Carter*. "As one of the only black girls in [the] country music scene, I hope Bey decides to sprinkle me with a dash of her magic," she wrote on social media in February 2024. Six weeks later, Adell and her fellow "Blackbiird" rising stars all saw their music streams surge. "It's absolutely seismic," she told NBC's *Today*. "The butterfly effect from this album will span probably the rest of our lives."

WESTERN WEAR: In the weeks following the album's release, sales of cowboy boots increased by 45 percent, as did Google searches for "cowboy hat" and "bolo tie." More specifically, Levi's—the title of *Cowboy Carter*'s seventeenth track, a collaboration with Post Malone—reported a 20 percent rise in its stock price as well as another 20 percent boost in foot traffic at US stores. In the UK, "women's Levi's jeans" surged 263 percent for British retailer John Lewis & Partners.

GRATEFUL EIGHT: *Cowboy Carter* is Beyoncé's eighth consecutive No. 1 album on the *Billboard* 200 and broke the record for first-day streams of a country album by a female artist on Amazon Music. Lead single "Texas Hold 'Em" topped both the Hot 100 and Hot Country Songs charts, making Bey the first Black woman to do so.

PART THREE

Beyoncé
A to Z

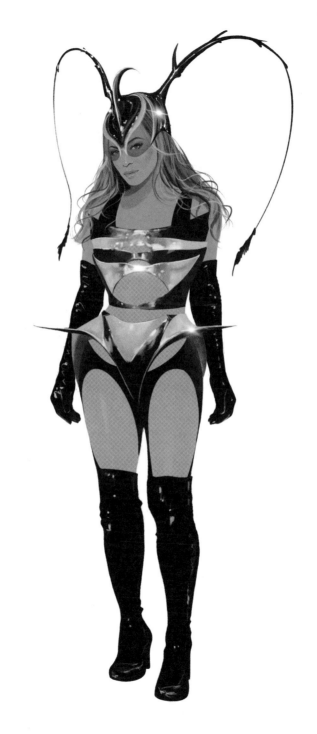

THE A-BEY-Cs
OF BEYONCÉ

Queen Bey puts the "buzz" in buzzword. The superstar's universe is so vast, there are endless fun facts for her devoted Hive members to discuss—and dissect. But to not bumble the conversation, you must have a firm grasp on *everything* about Beyoncé's music, business projects, favorite things, hidden talents, and hobbies. From her most impressive a cappella moments to the zodiac signs found in her lyrics, these are the A-Bey-Cs of Beyoncé everyone should know!

A CAPPELLA

Beyoncé is such an immense talent; she could sing the phonebook—and she wouldn't even need musical accompaniment! Countless times over her career, the Queen has proven her exceptional vocal gifts with a cappella renditions of songs. In 2000, as drama within Destiny's Child overshadowed Beyoncé, Kelly, and Michelle, the trio harmonized the chorus of "Say My Name" while presenting Best Male Video at the *MTV Video Music Awards*. As a solo artist, she stunned with a cover of Rose Royce's 1977 ballad, "Wishing on a Star," in the 2004 television ad campaign for Tommy Hilfiger's True Star fragrance.

In 2013, amid speculation that she had lip-synched the national anthem at Barack Obama's presidential inauguration, Bey silenced her critics at a press conference for her upcoming NFL Super Bowl Halftime Show performance. "Would you guys mind standing?" she asked the room of reporters. The screen behind her displayed the American flag, and for the next two minutes, the powerhouse perfected "The Star-Spangled Banner" in a room so quiet you could have heard a pin drop. After nailing it, she just wanted to know: "Any questions?"

Renaissance has been celebrated for its dance music and self-assured lyrics, and interestingly, Bey separated the two by releasing a cappella and instrumental versions of several songs. There's no question which one fans prefer: on YouTube, the a cappella rendition of "Break My Soul" has twice as many views as its music-only counterpart.

BEYCHELLA

For two weekends in April 2018, Beyoncé was the Queen of the Desert as headliner of the Coachella Music and Arts Festival—better known as

"Beychella." More importantly, the superstar was the first Black woman to receive top billing, a historic moment she celebrated onstage with more than one hundred musicians, singers, and dancers from Historically Black Colleges and Universities (HBCUs). "When I decided to do Coachella, instead of me pulling out my flower crown, it was more important that I brought our culture to Coachella," Bey explained in *Homecoming*, the Grammy-winning documentary that chronicled her Coachella experience.

The twenty-six-song Beychella setlist highlighted the greatest hits of her career, which of course owes a debt of gratitude to Destiny's Child. To rightfully pay homage, the superstar brought out Kelly Rowland and Michelle Williams—in matching ensembles, no less—for a medley of "Lose My Breath," "Say My Name," and "Soldier," stunning the 125,000 in attendance at the Indio, California, festival (and 41 million around the globe watching the livestream). Two other people who have supported Bey along the way, her husband, Jay-Z and sister, Solange, also joined her onstage for "Déjà Vu" and "Get Me Bodied," respectively.

The following year, fans got to relive the magic with *Homecoming*, a 2019 Netflix concert film that went behind the scenes of Beyoncé's eight-month preparation for Coachella, her first performance since giving birth to twins Rumi and Sir in 2017. Nearly a year after its premiere, *Homecoming* had a revival when fans organized a virtual rewatch party on March 18, 2020, to mitigate the stress of self-isolation during the COVID-19 lockdown. Bey may have also joined in from her own couch: she reposted the original tweet suggesting the idea—thus making it go viral.

CRAZY ARCHIVE

Since 2005, Bey has had her own personal "visual director" to document everyday life, sometimes up to sixteen hours a day. The behind-the-scenes footage has added exclusivity to her autobiographical films such as *Year of 4* and *Renaissance*—and it was easy to access, thanks to what the singer calls her "crazy archive." Modeled after NBC's digital library, Beyoncé's database catalogues all content with dates and enough pertinent information for cross-referencing. "You know, I can always say, 'I want that interview I did for *GQ*,' and we can find it," she explained to the magazine in 2013.

The archive, located inside a temperature-controlled facility at her home, contains every trace of her career: every photograph (dating back to Destiny's Child), every video of every performance, every interview, every digital diary—and it's all under the protection of security cameras and microphones. According to British tabloid *The Sun*, there's even a librarian.

"She's smart because she realized the value of owning her own footage," Bey's visual director Ed Burke told *Out* in 2014. At the time, a decade on since he began documenting her life, he revealed that the superstar had "backed off a bit" from the marathon sessions. "We still have a videographer, but the access isn't quite as crazy."

DUBAI

It was invitation-only when Bey performed her first show in five years on January 21, 2023, to celebrate the opening of Atlantis The Royal hotel in Dubai. The seventeen-song set opened with "At Last" and highlighted many of her greatest hits such as "Drunk in Love," "Halo," "Naughty

"She's smart because she realized the value of owning her own footage."

Girl"—and her daughter Blue Ivy. The eleven-year-old made her stage debut, singing and dancing alongside her mother for "Brown Skin Girl" while decked out in a red glittery costume. The moment went viral on social media, despite the event's strict no-filming policy (guests were given special pouches to lock their phones so "that you enjoy this once in a lifetime show").

The exclusive performance was indeed a night to remember, beginning with Bey's introduction: a sparkling bridge of waterfall lights in the sky over the Atlantis, created by five hundred pyro drones—and ending with the singer ascending sixteen feet (5 m) above the stage as a stunning shower of water and fireworks danced around her. The extravaganza was brought to life by Middle Eastern artists: Dubai-based fashion designers created Bey's lavish costume changes, and she was backed by an all-female Lebanese dance group and all-female local orchestra.

For the hour-long performance, Beyoncé earned a reported $24 million—that comes out to $400,000 a minute!—making it the highest-paying private concert in history, according to *Forbes*.

EAT, PLAY, LOVE

Did you know that Beyoncé is also an award-winning journalist? In 2011, the singer penned an essay for *Essence* called, "Eat, Play, Love," chronicling her nine-month hiatus following years of non-stop working. After wrapping the I Am . . . World Tour, she promised herself time "to do the things I never get to do. Simple things like play with my nephew, pick him up from school, visit museums, go to concerts, see some Broadway shows, learn to cook a meal, and spend time with my husband. My priority was savoring every moment," wrote Bey. "I was looking for tiny moments that would speak to my heart and make me smile."

Pairing her love of music and desire to travel, she attended concerts in London, Scotland, Tennessee, and Palm Springs to see diverse acts ranging from Stevie Wonder to rock band Rage Against the Machine. For the first time in her life, Beyoncé had time to explore countries she had only stopped in while on tour. After five weeks in Australia ("a carefree existence for me"), she headed to Japan, "where it was my idea to go unrecognized as a Harajuku girl—the young Japanese women who dress up like anime characters or in exaggerated gothic costumes." In London, she met one of her favorite singers, Sade; In Russia, she saw the ballet, *Swan Lake*; In Paris, she had escargot for lunch, "and it was actually tasty." And what would be a trip to Italy without pizza and red wine?

The experience gifted Beyoncé with a creative reawakening and new musical influences, which she applied to her next album, 4—critically acclaimed as her most accomplished to date. In 2012, "Eat, Play, Love" was recognized by the New York Association of Black Journalists (NYABJ). "Beyoncé is a role model," said NYABJ president, Michael Feeney. "I hope this honor will inspire other girls to pursue a career in journalism."

FRAGRANCE EMPIRE

After promoting Tommy Hilfiger's True Star and Emporio Armani's Diamonds perfumes, Beyoncé entered the fragrance market with her own signature scent, Heat, in 2010. True to its name, the commercial was red-hot: It opens with the singer nude and dripping in sweat as she sings Peggy Lee's 1958 jazz classic, "Fever" (Bey's cover also appeared on the five-song CD, *Heat*, which contained previously unreleased music). Consequently, the sexy ad was banned from daytime broadcast in the UK. Heat—a floral, fruity, and woody scent marketed as "feminine and irresistible"—came in an antique-style bottle designed to mimic a flame. "It's hot, it's sexy," described Bey. "It definitely makes you feel like you caught the fever." Fans indeed had a burning desire for Heat—seventy-two thousand bottles were sold in a single hour at the Macy's launch party.

Over the next six years, Bey's fragrance empire spread like wildfire, spawning seven additional scents: Heat Rush, Midnight Heat Heat Wild Orchid, Heat Kissed, Heat Seduction, and the limited-edition, Heat: The Mrs. Carter Show World Tour. There was also Pulse, inspired by her alter ego, Sasha Fierce, and Rise, in honor of Maya Angelou. By 2013, Beyoncé was one of the world's best-selling celebrity perfumers with a $400 million brand. A decade later, she launched her own Beyoncé Parfums, debuting with Cé Noir (This Black), created in France by the singer and "encased in art" in a sleek chrome bottle. The signature scent, with top notes of clementine and golden honey, is so exclusive that the only place to get it is Beyonce.com.

GUINNESS WORLD RECORDS

Bey holds at least twenty titles spanning music, wealth, and social media in the *Guinness World Records* books. Her earliest record dates back to 2010, when she earned ten Grammy nominations in a single year for her album *I Am . . . Sasha Fierce*. In 2014, she picked up three world record titles for earnings, including the highest earnings for a female in a single year ($115 million), a record she set again in 2022. Her 2018 Coachella headlining gig lit up Twitter (now known as X), where she took the title for the most average retweets for a female musician (31,615 in a day). Four years later with *Renaissance*, Bey became the only act to debut at No. 1 with their first seven studio albums. As of 2023, the Queen holds the world record for the most wins ever at the *Grammys* (32), *MTV Music Video Awards* (29), and *BET Awards* (35)—and the same year she was rightfully inducted into the Guinness World Records Hall of Fame.

One member of the BeyHive holds a Guinness World Record herself: UK broadcaster, Clara Amfo, successfully identified twelve Beyoncé songs in one minute simply by hearing a lyric during BBC Radio 1's 2021 LOL-a-Thon charity event.

*"We share a philosophy
that puts creativity, growth,
and social responsibility
at the forefront of business."*

HOUSE OF DERÉON

Destiny's Child made bold Y2K fashion statements with their coordinating
ensembles, all created by stylist Tina Knowles. Fans wanted to follow
the trendsetters, so in 2006, Beyoncé and her mother launched House
of Deréon. A ready-to-wear line that mixed hip-hop style with feminine
accents, it is described as the intersection "where the sidewalk and catwalk
meet." Named after Tina's mother, Agnèz Deréon, a seamstress, there were
plenty of vintage influences found in the line's pencil skirts and 1950s
dresses. "We wanted to take elements from my grandmother's legacy—the
beaded lace, lush colors, fine fabrics—and mix them with clothes from my
mother's generation and my generation," Bey dished to *Ebony*.

As House of Deréon expanded to footwear and handbags, so did its reach: Originally only sold in US department stores, the fashion brand headed overseas in 2009 to open its first location in South Korea. Two years later, Beyoncé and Tina showed their Autumn/Winter collection at London Fashion Week and secured a deal with the upscale Selfridges, a United Kingdom-based department store chain. "It's been such a great journey," Bey said at the 2011 launch, a year before House of Deréon went out of style for good. "It's beautiful because we're family and because it's more than just a clothing line—it's part of our life."

IVY PARK

After House of Deréon, Beyoncé shifted her fashion focus to her own line, Ivy Park. Named after her daughter Blue Ivy and Houston's Parkwood Park—where she exercised in her youth—the athleisure collection launched in 2014 as a joint venture with the company Topshop. However, four years later, when Topshop's Sir Philip Green was accused of sexual harassment and racial abuse, Bey's Parkwood Entertainment acquired total ownership of the brand. In 2019, she found a new partner, Adidas, a company with "tremendous success in pushing creative boundaries," Bey excitedly announced. "We share a philosophy that puts creativity, growth, and social responsibility at the forefront of business. I look forward to re-launching and expanding Ivy Park on a truly global scale with a proven, dynamic leader."

But the world was about to face unforeseen circumstances. In January 2020, Ivy Park's debut collection sold out in six minutes and media analysts predicted it would exceed Adidas' most profitable collaboration with Kanye West's $1.5-billion Yeezy collection. Just two months later, COVID-19

sparked a global lockdown that impacted future sales: Ivy Park made only $93 million in 2021 and plummeted further to $40 million in 2022. That year, after Bey received her guaranteed fees, Adidas actually lost $10 million. In March 2023, the retailer and superstar agreed to part ways with the fashion line. Legends never die, of course. "The PARK lives forever," the brand declared on social media, after dropping its final Adidas collaboration—the all-black Ivy Park Noir. "A new era awaits."

JOY

After three decades of grinding nonstop, Bey looked ahead to her forties with one word that became her mantra: joy. Reflecting on how the COVID-19 lockdown slowed down her life and allowed more time with family, Bey decided to "shed stressful things," she told British *Vogue* in 2020. "I released *Lemonade* during the Formation World Tour, gave birth to twins, performed at Coachella, directed *Homecoming*, went on another world tour with Jay, then *Black Is King*, all back-to-back. It's been heavy and hectic . . . Now, I've decided to give myself permission to focus on my joy."

The following year, she expanded on her wish for the next decade in an interview with *Harper's Bazaar*. Although she gave no indication that she was about to drop *Renaissance*, if you read between the lines, her new outlook hinted at spreading peace through her music (and subsequent world tour): "I want to travel without working. I want this next decade to be about celebration, joy, and giving and receiving love. I want to give all the love I have to the people who love me back."

KARAOKE FAN

Beyoncé has sold out stadiums all over the world, but she's not above hopping on the mic at a local karaoke bar—just don't expect an impromptu performance of "Bootylicious." In fact, her go-to songs are not even in the same genre as her music: "Escape (The Piña Colada Song)"—yes, that one—and "Hotel California" by 1970s rockers The Eagles. "The guitar solo is my jam," Bey revealed in a 2019 Ask Me Anything interview published in *Elle*. Years earlier, she recalled the time that she, Kelly, and Michelle goofed off at a karaoke bar with a silly rendition of "I Will Survive" by Gloria Gaynor. "We weren't singing for real, of course. But everybody was like, 'Wow. Destiny's Child sounds really bad!'"

In 2014, the trio surprised a group of fans attempting to perform Beyoncé's "Party" at Sing Sing karaoke bar in Miami. The professionals were in a VIP room with Jay-Z and producer Timbaland when they heard the familiar sound of Bey's 2011 track. "I want to see who's singing my song," she told owner Kellie Pilicer, who recounted the wild night to *Us Weekly*. "Beyoncé and Michelle started singing and dancing with them. These girls had no idea it was them for the first couple of minutes." One unfortunate fan never did figure it out. In security footage from inside the karaoke room, a partied-out friend can be seen sleeping on the couch, with Beyoncé and Kelly photobombing her in a series of pictures.

LION KING

The singer redefined childhood nostalgia when she lent her voice to the 2019 photorealistic remake of Disney's animated classic *The Lion King*. As Nala, Simba's childhood-friend-turned-love-interest Beyoncé empowered the character to be more than simply a sidekick. In the reimagining, it was

"She's a unique talent, to say the least."

important that "the females in this film were heroes," with Nala alongside Simba, Bey told *Good Morning America*. "I thought that was very interesting and very real, because the women are, you know, we're the fighters." Bey also shaped the evolution of Nala. After director Jon Favreau attended the On the Run II Tour, "it gave me ideas," he revealed to *Entertainment Weekly*. "As I've been directing the animation for the past couple of years, ideas have cropped up for me seeing what she was doing as a performer and how that could inform the character that she plays."

For Favreau, Bey was his first and only choice to play Nala. When the project was announced in 2017, she was pregnant with twins and the filmmaker guaranteed they would do whatever was necessary to accommodate her complicated schedule. "I've got the BeyHive in my house," he joked to *EW*. "She's a unique talent, to say the least. And when I finally spoke to her after reaching out, although her persona onstage is bigger than life, she's very down to earth and is very much dedicated to her family and having a life that is human-scale."

It wouldn't be a musical without Beyoncé's famous pipes. In addition to recording a modern rendition of "Can You Feel the Love Tonight" with Donald Glover (Simba), Seth Rogen (Pumbaa), and Billy Eichner (Timon), the superstar created a second soundtrack, *The Lion King: The Gift*, composed of additional new songs inspired by the remake, featuring musicians and producers from Africa, where the film is set. "I wanted to put everyone on their own journey to link the storyline," explained Bey. "Each song was written to reflect the film's storytelling that gives the listener a chance to imagine their own imagery while listening to a new contemporary interpretation."

MAIDEN NAME

When Destiny's Child arrived on the scene back in 1997, no one had ever heard of Beyoncé or the name itself. That's because it's actually a misspelling of her mother's maiden name, Beyince. The youngest of seven children, Tina's birth certificate incorrectly cites her surname as "Beyoncé." It stuck, and when her first daughter was born in 1981, Tina wanted her maiden name to continue on—even if her family was not thrilled with the honor. "My dad said, 'She's gonna be real mad at you, because that's a last name,'" Tina recalled to *Rolling Stone* in 2004. "And I'm like, 'It's not a last name to anybody but you guys.'"

As it turned out, Beyoncé's grandfather wasn't exactly wrong as the unique moniker did welcome bullying at school. "Through the years, I've grown to love it, but when I was little, it was just another reason for kids to pick on me," Bey revealed in the Destiny's Child memoir, *Soul Survivors*. "Every morning when the teacher would take roll, I wanted to crawl under my desk."

These days, now that everyone in the world knows Beyoncé, it's Tina who sometimes raises eyebrows. Her passport reads "Tina Beyoncé" just like her birth certificate. "People say, 'Oh how did you change your name to her name?' I'm like, that's my name! She got my name. I had it first," Tina joked on the red carpet of the 2021 *Billboard Music Awards*. "I'm the original Beyoncé!"

NET WORTH

On "Pure/Honey," Bey sings about how much it should cost to look the way she does, and after the Renaissance World Tour, she's well on her way to ten figures. According to *Forbes*, as of December 2023, the superstar's net worth is an estimated $800 million. Just six months earlier, Beyoncé was ranked No. 48 on the business magazine's richest celebrities list with $540 million. But her blockbuster summer tour elevated everything. In addition to her gaining $100 million in post-tax earnings, *Forbes* adjusted her music catalog to $300 million. The remainder of her $800 million fortune is split between business holdings and personal assets shared with husband Jay-Z, who is worth $2.5 billion himself, and is one of only fourteen Black billionaires in the world (including Oprah Winfrey, Rihanna, Tiger Woods, and Tyler Perry).

OBAMA FAMILY SUPERFANS

The BeyHive is filled with celebrity fans, but it doesn't get much more A-list than Barack and Michelle Obama. Bey's relationship with the former first couple dates back to 2009, when she sang, "At Last," as they danced at the Inaugural Ball; she said it was "one of the biggest moments of my life" up to that point. Four years later, when the President was reelected,

Beyoncé returned to Washington, D.C. to conclude his 2013 inauguration ceremony with the National Anthem.

"She's a sweetheart," the First Lady gushed during a 2016 appearance on *The Late Show With Stephen Colbert*. "She's smart, she's creative, she's a great mother, she loves her family. She's just a low-key lady. So we have a lot in common in that way—except I can't sing, I can't dance." But that didn't stop her from trying. Mrs. Obama belted every word of "Single Ladies" (and perfected Bey's iconic hand twirl) on James Corden's *Carpool Karaoke*. "We were both fully in the BeyHive," remarked *The Late Late Show* host as they stopped to catch their breaths. "We were making honey," she joked, ". . . to put in our *Lemonade!*"

Civilian life only gave the Obamas more freedom to enjoy Beyoncé's music. Michelle attended the On the Run II Tour twice—in Paris with her youngest daughter Sasha and again in Washington, D.C. with Barack. Although they weren't spotted at the Renaissance Tour, the couple are fans of her latest album. Barack put "America Has a Problem," Bey's politically charged collaboration with Kendrick Lamar, on his Favorite Music of 2023 list. His wife publicly wished the superstar a happy forty-second birthday that September. "Your talent and music have brought so much joy to all of our lives," Michelle shared on social media (along with the crown and bee emojis). "You're truly one-of-one, and I'm just so proud of you."

PLANT-BASED DIET

Like she sings on "Cozy," Bey is comfortable in her own skin. She nourishes her body with a plant-based diet that's more about feeding her soul than shedding pounds. Her meals consist of fiber-rich vegetables, fruits, whole grains, legumes, nuts, and seeds. The singer and her husband first made the decision to "go vegan" by cutting out meat and dairy back in 2013 when they took part in Marcos Borges's 22-Day Challenge, a program that promises to "transform your body, reset your habits, and change your life" through a plant-based diet in twenty-two days. For Beyoncé, the challenge started with one vegan meal a day, typically breakfast. According to Borges, the Carters have a private chef who whips up some of their favorites: overnight oats, avocado toast, and a meat replacement made of raw walnuts combined with spices, vinegar, and coconut aminos.

Bey was hooked from the start, often Instagramming snapshots of her delicious meals with the hashtag #22DayVeganChallenge. In 2015, she and Jay-Z partnered with Borges for the 22-Day Nutrition, a plant-based meal-delivery service to bring the revolutionary health program to fans. "This is something I have to share with everyone," Bey announced on *Good Morning America*. "I have struggled since a young age with diets and finding something that actually works."

More so, she and Jay-Z are particularly drawn to plant-based nutrition for the sustainability of the planet, according to Borges, who met the couple through Pharrell Williams. In 2017, the guru and author of *The Greenprint*—the name noticeably similar to Jay-Z's *The Blueprint*—launched a website that allows people to track the amount of water, trees, and carbon emissions saved with each vegan meal they eat. The Carters were so inspired by the data, they came up with an idea to get people to take the plant-based pledge: Concert Tickets for Life, a program that awarded a lucky fan who committed to eating at least one vegan meal a day with Beyoncé and Jay-Z tickets for "life" (technically, thirty years). Bey practices what she preaches. She adheres to daily plant-based breakfasts and Meatless Mondays.

QUEEN BEE(KEEPER)

Sometimes life imitates art. After years of being known as Queen Bey by her dedicated legion of fans, the BeyHive, the superstar embraced the nickname, literally. "I know it's random, but I have two beehives. Real ones," she told British *Vogue* in 2020. "I've had them at my house for a while now. I have around eighty thousand bees and we make hundreds of jars of honey a year. I started the beehives because my daughters, Blue and Rumi, both have terrible allergies, and honey has countless healing properties." The following year, Bey—who also discovered CBD to treat inflammation and insomnia—revealed she was building a hemp and honey farm. "I have so much to share," she teased, "and there's more to come soon!" However, as of 2024, fans are still buzzing for the sweet details.

REAL ESTATE PORTFOLIO

From coast to coast, Beyoncé and Jay-Z live large. The billion-dollar couple started small (for them): an eight thousand-square-foot (743 m²) penthouse in New York's Tribeca, which the rapper bought for $6.85 million during his bachelor days. After getting married, their first joint purchase was a $7 million Mediterranean-style villa on the exclusive, celeb-friendly island Indian Creek Village in Miami. Two years later, the Carters flipped the property and headed back to New York, specifically the Hamptons, where they own Pond House, a $26 million five-bedroom cottage surrounded by a 17½-acre (7 ha) nature preserve. Inside, the craftsmanship is museum-quality—and all done by hand: Italian marble bathtubs carved from single blocks of stone, Parquet de Versailles floorboards installed by French artisans, and quarter-sawn white-oak paneling with a French chalk finish.

"You see the one that really wants it. It was so entertaining, the energy, seeing the girls battle ... God, it was the best. It was magical."

In Los Angeles, Queen Bey became the fresh princess of Bel-Air in 2017, when she and Jay-Z invested $88 million—the most expensive transaction in the city that year—in a modern mansion with eleven bathrooms, four pools, and a fifteen-car garage. Six years later, the Carters set a California record with the purchase of a $200 million home in Malibu, the most expensive ever sold in the state (and second in the entire country). The thirty thousand-square-foot (2,787 m²) beachfront property sits on its own bluff in the Paradise Cove area, better known as Billionaires' Row.

SUGA MAMA

Who runs Beyoncé's world tours? Girls. Before she hit the road for The Beyoncé Experience in 2006, Beyoncé formed an all-female band dubbed

Suga Mama, after her song on *B'Day*. Auditions were held in Atlanta, Chicago, Houston, and Los Angeles to fill nine musician slots, including percussionists, guitarists, and saxophonists. The competition was so stiff, tryouts quickly turned into a battle of the bands. "I brought in two of every instrument and that's how I chose," Bey told MTV News. "You see the one that really wants it. It was so entertaining, the energy, seeing the girls battle . . . God, it was the best. It was magical."

Suga Mama was so sweet, the band was featured in several of Bey's music videos, as well as her performances at the 2013 Super Bowl and Michelle Obama's fiftieth birthday party. Over the years, members have moved on to other projects, but three original Suga Mamas were with Beyoncé as recently as the Renaissance Tour: trumpeter Crystal Rovél Torres, saxophonist Katty Rodriguez-Harrold, and vocalist Tiffany Monique Ryan.

TIFFANY DIAMOND

In 2021, Beyoncé made history as the first Black woman to ever wear the iconic 128.54-carat Tiffany Diamond, considered an American crown jewel. As the face of Tiffany & Co's "About Love" campaign with Jay-Z, she modeled the 150-year-old rock popularized by Audrey Hepburn during the 1961 promotional tour for *Breakfast at Tiffany's*—clad in a black gown and opera gloves à la Holly Golightly, no less. In another nod to the Golden Age actress, Bey sang "Moon River" in a video advertisement by Emmanuel Adjei, who directed her musical film *Black Is King*.

The singer was only the fourth woman to ever wear the Tiffany Diamond, which was discovered in 1877 and first exhibited at the 1893 Chicago World's Fair. American socialite Mary Whitehouse debuted the jewel, one of the world's largest yellow diamonds, at the 1957 Tiffany Ball. After Hepburn, the diamond was not worn again for nearly sixty years, until Tiffany loaned the $30 million bauble to Best Actress nominee Lady Gaga, for the 2019 *Academy Awards*. After she won the Oscar for Best Original Song, "I just left with the diamond on and I didn't tell anyone," she revealed on *The Graham Norton Show*. "Tiffany's started freaking out." Security eventually caught up to Gaga at a Taco Bell "and it was very politely removed from my neck."

UNCLE JOHNNY

One of the biggest inspirations for the *Renaissance* album is Beyoncé's Uncle Johnny, her mother's best friend and "the most fabulous gay man I have ever met." Growing up, Johnny was a fixture around the Knowles household and helped raise Beyoncé and Solange. He drove the sisters to school, made their clothes (like Bey's prom dress!), and influenced their uniqueness. The girls worshipped their Uncle Johnny, and when he died from AIDS in 1998 "they took it hard," remembered Tina, who was actually Johnny's aunt (her older sister was his mother).

His spirit lives on throughout *Renaissance*, and in a special shoutout on "Heated," a song about feeling red-hot in Chanel, Hermès, and Ivy Park. When Tina heard the lyric, "I got so teary eyed," she revealed on Instagram. "You see Johnny loved house music! And introduced my kids to it early on. He is smiling from Heaven at Bey right now!"

The singer previously honored Uncle Johnny in 2019 when she received the GLAAD Vanguard Award. Watching him suffer from AIDS "was one of the most painful experiences," she said, fighting back tears. "He lived his truth, he was brave and unapologetic during a time when this

"He lived his truth, he was brave and unapologetic during a time when this country wasn't as accepting . . ."

country wasn't as accepting . . . I'm hopeful that his struggle served to open pathways for other young people to live more freely."

VOCAL RANGE

One of the most powerful and distinct voices in music, Bey's talent is off the charts. According to experts, she has a vocal range believed to be between 3.5 and 4 octaves—but precisely which notes she spans is up for debate. While most agree her highest is F6, her lowest note depends on the ear. Other 4-octave contemporaries include Lady Gaga, Christina Aguilera, Ariana Grande, and Paramore's Hayley Williams. For comparison, Mariah Carey is one of the few living singers with a vocal range of 5 octaves.

Bey's voice type is mezzo-soprano: higher than alto (low register) but lower than soprano (highest register). But for 2019's *The Lion King: The Gift* soundtrack, she showed off her seldom-heard operatic mezzo-soprano.

"I started taking voice lessons from an opera singer at nine," she revealed to *Harper's Bazaar*. "I had my first vocal injury at thirteen from singing in the studio for too many hours. We had just gotten our first record deal, and I was afraid I had developed nodules and destroyed my voice and that my career could be over. The doctors put me on vocal rest all summer."

In 2023, *Rolling Stone* named Beyoncé No. 8 on its list of 200 Greatest Singers of All Time—behind Mariah (No. 5), Billie Holiday (No. 4), Whitney Houston (No. 2), and Aretha Franklin (No. 1). "In Beyoncé's voice lies the entire history of Black music," praised the music bible. "At times brashly Southern or cherubically hymnal, her malleability and penchant for vocal theatricals have allowed her range to successfully fit into everything from funk to country to hard rock, sometimes all on the same album"—most notably, *Lemonade*.

WALK OF FAME

The first unofficial Destiny's Child reunion came on March 28, 2006, when the trio was honored with a star on the Hollywood Walk of Fame. It rained the day of the ceremony, but fans still swarmed the Hollywood Boulevard landmark to see Beyoncé, Kelly, and Michelle receive the distinction for their contributions to the recording industry. "Dreams come true," Bey told the crowd. Kelly recalled their first trip to Hollywood and seeing the Walk of Fame, a popular attraction that draws over ten million tourists each year: "We were like, 'We want a star.' To be here is so humbling and we are so honored." Destiny's Child's star, located in front of the Dolby Theatre (venue for the annual Academy Awards), is the 2,035th to be embedded along the 1.3-mile (2.1 km) historic landmark.

X BALMAIN

Bey doesn't just collaborate in the music studio. She's worked with Olivier Rousteing, creative director of French fashion house Balmain, on several couture collections. The two geniuses first came together for Bey's headline gig at the 2018 Coachella festival. Rousteing custom-designed the singer's iconic wardrobe for her two-weekend performance, as well as hundreds of costumes for her dancers and musicians—and fans got the chance to own a piece of pop culture history with Beyoncé x Balmain. The three-piece capsule collection offered similar pink and yellow hoodies with a sorority-inspired graphic she wore onstage (starting at $595), as well as a more moderately-priced $290 T-shirt with the same logo. It was a fashion investment for a good cause as proceeds were donated to the United Negro College Fund.

Bey and Rousteing made history again for Renaissance Couture. Inspired by her experimental album, the duo brought each track to life with an avant-garde fashion piece—the first wearable album. "Alien Superstar" is a 3D structured gown and headpiece; "Cozy," a black velvet dress with pink feathers; and "I'm That Girl," a hammered metal spiked bustier. Bey modeled "Heated," a thermoformed black velvet gown and hat set with crystals, on the April 2023 cover of French *Vogue*.

Renaissance Couture was born the moment Rousteing hit play on the new album. "It's a beautiful thing, the act of sketching, guided only by rhythm, music, and lyrics . . . just by ear," he told the magazine. After months of Zoom meetings with Bey going over the details of each piece, the designer brought the finished collection from Paris to a Los Angeles recording studio, where he styled everything on mannequins. "We had been transported to a world of couture in this big, dark space," he recalled. "She said, 'This is a museum, couture pieces . . . This will stay forever.'"

YONCÉ

Sasha Fierce isn't the only alter ego Beyoncé has showcased over the years. In 2013, Mrs. Carter introduced Yoncé, a feisty head-turner, in the lyrics of "Partition." The nickname was actually coined by her producer, The-Dream, during a freestyling session with Bey and Justin Timberlake in the recording studio. "It was really organic, and it reminded me of being in middle school during the lunch breaks," she told fans at a *Beyoncé* visual album screening. "And Dream just started, 'Yoncé on his mouth like liquor,' and I'm like, 'What does that mean?' But I love it."

Yoncé is who all women want to be, and all men want to be with, according to the partially-rapped verses in what *Billboard* describes as "a lady-thug anthem." The two-minute ditty ends with the click of paparazzi cameras that transitions the track into the "Partition" portion of the song. "Yoncé" took on a life of its own as it eventually moved from the song to a separate visual featuring supermodels Chanel Iman, Joan Smalls, and Jourdan Dunn.

To capture the essence of Yoncé—described by director, Ricky Saiz, as "someone you talk about"—the super-sexy video mimics the song's aggressive aesthetic: lots of skin, leather, fishnets, and most memorably, a shot of Smalls licking Beyoncé's chest. "She almost plays like a madam character and the girls are doing the performing for her in a sense," Saiz explained to MTV News. "[It's] almost like this just happened and we were there with our cameras."

*"I have high expectations of myself
and expect the exact same thing
of everyone around me."*

ZODIAC SIGNS

Born on September 4, Beyoncé is a Virgo: hardworking, artistic, analytical, and destined for perfectionism. "I am a Virgo to the tee!" she admitted to *Dazed and Confused* magazine. "I like to think outside the box. I don't believe in the answer 'no'. I am extremely driven and extremely critical—sometimes overly critical. Sometimes it is one of the things that I have to work on. I am a control freak. I pay attention to details. When I do something, I do it 100 percent. I have high expectations of myself and expect the exact same thing of everyone around me. I've always been that way. I am all or nothing."

Bey is so into her zodiac sign, she's written several odes about it, beginning with "Gift From Virgo," a love ballad on 2003's *Dangerously in*

Love. The album also features "Signs," which gives a shoutout to all twelve houses in astrology—sexy Scorpios, fun Libras, flirtatious Aries—as she determines who best suits her affectionate Virgo personality. When the song was released, she still hadn't confirmed her relationship with Jay-Z, but the lyrics gave a pretty solid hint as she sang about loving a Saggitarius, the rapper's sign. "People can come to whatever conclusion they like," Bey would only tell MTV News. "That's the beauty of music."

During her *Renaissance* era, Bey was all about celebrating the sixth sign of the zodiac. The 2022 album's fourth single, "Virgo's Groove," is a disco-funk track that took several years to perfect—just like a Virgo! For her forty-second birthday, in 2023, the superstar dropped an official "Virgo's Groove" Renaissance World Tour T-shirt. As a gift to herself, she asked fans to wear "your most fabulous silver fashions" to her shows during the month of September: "Virgo season together in the House of Chrome."

PART FOUR

Renaissance Woman

WORKER BEY

In 2010, after nearly two decades of being managed by her father, Mathew Knowles, Beyoncé decided to end their working relationship and handle all business herself. She established Parkwood Entertainment, named after the street she grew up on in Houston. It serves as an umbrella for her various brands in music, film, and fashion. The company quickly evolved from its original purpose as a production unit for her films *Cadillac Records* (2008, Tristar Pictures) and *Obsessed* (2009, Sony Pictures) into a full-fledged operation that includes a record label—not only for her own music and videos but also as management for fellow artists like Chloe x Halle, whom she signed in 2015 after their cover of "Pretty Hurts" went viral.

Looking back on her career as she turned forty, "I took control of my independence at twenty-seven and started Parkwood Entertainment," Bey reminisced to *Harper's Bazaar* in 2021. "At the time, there wasn't a company that did what I needed it to do or ran the way I wanted it to run. So, I created this multipurpose badass conglomerate that was a creative agency, record label, production company, and management company to produce and work on projects that meant the most to me. I wanted to manage myself and have a company that put art and creativity first."

And that proved to be a commercial success! As the guiding light of her music career, the singer pulled off one of the biggest shocks in entertainment history when she dropped 2013's *Beyoncé* without warning. It's even more jaw-dropping that she had also created a music video for each of the seventeen tracks, inventing the idea of a visual album that has since been replicated by the likes of Kanye West (now known simply as Ye), Ed Sheeran, and Halsey—but not nearly on the same level as the Queen's self-titled masterpiece. For the trailblazer, it was a risky move but also record-breaking: *Beyoncé* sold nearly one million copies worldwide in its first three days, making it the fastest-selling album in the history of the iTunes Store at the time.

But she didn't do it alone. "I found a team of underdogs, a team of women, a team of people that no one believed in and we worked together," the superstar told fans during a *Beyoncé* Q&A session in New York. "And we

*"I found a team of underdogs,
a team of women, a team of people
that no one believed in
and we worked together."*

stayed up all night and we were progressive and we did not follow the rules. We said, 'Why can't we do it?' And I don't think people believed. I said to so many people, 'I have an idea to do a visual album and I want to . . .' And they were like, 'uhhhh, okay . . .' And we did it. Not only did we do it. It's my company and I'm very proud of that."

Parkwood Entertainment came a long way fairly quickly. One of her first decisions as CEO was to move the company from Houston to New York, and the early days were more like a shoestring operation than a multimillionaire's enterprise. "I just have memories of when there was no air conditioning in the new building and we didn't have an office, and it was like camping," Bey recalled in a 2013 interview with *The Gentlewoman*. "It was like, 'If you want to be a part of this, you got to grind it out.' It's a different level of commitment because it comes from love and respect, and that's how I try to lead. I think about Madonna and how she took all of the great things she achieved, started the label, and developed other artists. But there are not enough of those women."

And it wasn't just lip service. After signing Chloe x Halle to a $1 million contract, Bey brought the Bailey sisters on the road as her opening act for 2016's The Formation Tour and On the Run II Tour with Jay-Z in 2018. Ever since, their careers have skyrocketed: Chloe x Halle opened the 2019 Super Bowl with "America the Beautiful"; their debut album—which they cowrote and Chloe coproduced—received two Grammy nominations; and Halle starred in the 2023 live-action remake of Disney's *The Little Mermaid*. With Parkwood, the young artists not only have a global superstar as a mentor, but total creative freedom over their music. "Beyoncé understands," Chloe told *Rolling Stone* in 2021. "She just lets us spread our wings."

BEYONCÉ WITH THE GOOD HAIR

Like mother, like daughter! In February 2024, Beyoncé launched her own hair care brand, Cécred, based on what she learned growing up in Tina Knowles's Houston salon, where she swept floors after school. "I saw how she transformed hair by mixing mainstream products with textured haircare," Bey explains on cecred.com. "It's been my lifelong dream to create these hair products and bring some of my mother's teachings to life." Cécred (pronounced "sacred") offers shampoos, conditioners, masks, oils, and lotions all powered by the brand's own technology, Bioactive Keratin Ferment, which mimics keratin in human hair to repair and reinforce damaged strands. Beyoncé was a teenager when she first brought up the idea to her mother, who serves as vice chairwoman for Cécred. "She's a visionary and a brilliant woman and has worked so hard on this brand alongside me," she told *Essence*. "Honoring the legacy and the wisdom passed down through generations, and mixing it with science and technology, is part of this line. It was important that we borrowed some of our past and brought it into the future."

POP CULTURE ICON

Beyoncé has been breaking the Internet long before social media, memes, or Gen Z even existed. Since Y2K, she has kept the world riveted by her every move, whether it's collaborating with fellow icons like Britney Spears and Lady Gaga, announcing her pregnancy on live television, dropping a surprise album when half the world was asleep, defending a teenage Taylor Swift against Kanye West—and most recently, challenging the BeyHive to be on mute during the Renaissance Tour. These are Beyoncé's iconic moments engraved in the pop culture history books.

I LOVE WHALES

It was meant to be a sincere response. In 2001, Destiny's Child was being interviewed by Amsterdam's *Toazted* when the host tossed them a softball question: Suppose you could be an animal for one day; what would you pick? "That's hard," mused Kelly, as Beyoncé deadpanned, "I know what I'd be . . . a whale. I've loved whales since I was a little girl." Kelly chose a bird and Michelle a black panther—but all anyone could talk about was Beyoncé and her whale. Between the trio's kooky answers (in all fairness, it was a kooky question) and their burned-out demeanors, the perception was that Destiny's Child had enjoyed Amsterdam's cannabis culture prior to the interview.

Two decades later, video clips of Beyoncé saying "I love whales" can be found all over social media. During a 2019 Ask Me Anything for *Elle* magazine, one fan asked the singer the question weighing on everyone's minds: Would you still be a whale? "I still love whales," insisted Beyoncé. "And I love being in the ocean. And that video was after a sixteen-hour press day. Not marijuana!!"

WHEN BEYONCÉ RUINED CHRISTMAS

In the early 2000s, no celebrity was safe from Ashton Kutcher's MTV prank show, *Punk'd*. And for season 2's finale, it was Beyoncé's turn to get tricked on national television. Under the impression that she was the guest of honor at a holiday charity event for children, the singer smiles for the cameras as she stands on a forklift and places a star atop a thirty-foot (9 m) Christmas tree—when it topples over onto the crowd below. Screams can be heard, as elves and Santa race to rescue the living nativity scene actors trapped under the branches. Beyoncé, frozen from shock, looks on helplessly as one kid cries out, "You ruined our Christmas!" The mortified singer eventually descends to the holiday carnage and is confronted by the distraught children. "Why did you do that?" asks a little girl as Beyoncé apologizes. "What happened to our presents?" Event organizers also attempt to comfort the heartbroken little ones. "She didn't ruin it, she just wrecked it a lot," remarks a man within earshot of Bey, and then asks her for a photo. After what feels like an excruciating eternity, Ashton pops out to let her in on the joke.

Two decades later, we're still laughing: every year at the holidays, video clips titled "Beyoncé Ruins Christmas" resurface on social media.

POP TRINITY SLAY

In 2004, Pepsi brought together three of the most popular female voices in music for an epic commercial so cinematic that it received its own film premiere. "New Gladiator" starred pop rivals Beyoncé, Britney Spears, and Pink as female warriors set to fight to the death in a coliseum for the amusement of a Roman emperor, played by "Bailamos" singer Enrique Iglesias. The three-minute ad opens with the singers, dressed in scant armor, preparing for battle in separate underground chambers. As they hear the roar of the crowd, Beyoncé stands and thumps her weapon, a triton, on the ground, creating a beat that's carried on by Pink and Britney in nearby cells. It's a familiar sound: "We Will Rock You" by the band Queen. By the time the three enter the ring, they've decided to defy the emperor (who's sitting on his throne drinking a can of Pepsi). They lay down their weapons—and serenade the spectators with the 1977 rock anthem.

Pepsi spared no expense for its multimillion-dollar campaign, shot on location in Rome, albeit at a fake coliseum down the street from the real

"It's great to be in the presence of such great artists and entertainers, and I've been having the time of my life."

Coliseum. CGI was used to make it seem like Beyoncé, Britney, and Pink were performing to a crowd of fifty thousand people. Among the extras on set were Queen's Brian May and Roger Taylor, who were also hired to arrange the new version of "We Will Rock You."

The commercial debuted at London's National Gallery in Trafalgar Square, where Beyoncé, Britney, and Pink walked a blue carpet in honor of Pepsi's signature color. "It's great to be in the presence of such great artists and entertainers, and I've been having the time of my life," Bey gushed. "I got to fly all the way to Rome, which is one of the most beautiful places in the world."

THE TYRA INTERVIEW

Over the years, Beyoncé has been interviewed by some of the biggest journalists in history, from Oprah Winfrey to Barbara Walters. But it's her 2008 Q&A session on *The Tyra Banks Show* that goes down as the most legendary. Instead of asking "the same questions," the host switched it up for a segment called "Beyoncé My Name, Say My Name." For the next five minutes, Tyra rattled off a string of comically bad questions, in the form of puns, that grew increasingly bizarre.

Tyra asked, "Buy-oncé: When was the last time you bought something in the store?" Momentarily puzzled, the singer rebounded with an entertaining answer: twenty copies of her latest album, *I Am . . . Sasha Fierce*.

The next question got even stranger, as Tyra moved onto "Seanc-é: If you could communicate with anybody that has passed away, who would it be?" Bey didn't need to think long, revealing she would connect with her maternal grandmother, Agnèz Deréon.

However, she was slightly thrown by "Brie-yoncé: What's your favorite type of cheese?" With an awkward laugh, she offered, "regular yellow cheddar cheese."

But the wackiest was yet to come. The second round of questioning, related to Sasha Fierce, was next-level cringe: "Washa Fierce: Do you sing in the shower?" asked Tyra. Bey dissolved into giggles as she admitted, "It's so embarrassing, I definitely do."

Fifteen years later, Tyra stood by the widely mocked interview. "[Beyoncé] liked to have fun," she insisted to E! News, "so we were like, 'OK, you wanna have fun? Let's go.' And she just loved the crazy stuff that we would do."

KANYEGATE

The *MTV Video Music Awards* are notorious for watercooler moments—who can forget Madonna kissing Britney Spears and Christina Aguilera—but

"I didn't know this was going to happen, I feel so bad for her."

no one could have predicted Kanye West's reaction to Taylor Swift beating Beyoncé in 2009. As the nineteen-year-old singer accepted the award for Best Female Video ("You Belong With Me"), the rapper stormed the stage, grabbed her mic, and announced on live television why "Beyoncé had one of the best music videos of all time" with "Single Ladies." The camera then cut to Bey mortified in the audience. "Oh Kanye," she mouths in disbelief. The show went right to a commercial break as MTV producers scrambled to rectify the unprecedented situation.

Backstage, Taylor was in tears. Ye, as the rapper now calls himself, was immediately booted from Radio City Music Hall, but not before Pink gave him a piece of her mind (what she said is unclear, but "she was pointing in his face," according to MTV News correspondent James Montgomery). In the chaos, then-Viacom president Van Toffler recalled finding Beyoncé crying to her father. "She was like, 'I didn't know this was going to happen, I feel so bad for her.'" Toffler, who had prior knowledge of the night's winners, urged Bey to stay, revealing she would end up onstage to accept an award, "and perhaps this is a way to have this come full circle and let [Taylor] have her moment." Sure enough, when Beyoncé won Video of the Year, she graciously gave up her spotlight. "I remember being seventeen years old, up for my first MTV Award with Destiny's Child, and it was one of the most exciting moments in my life," she told the crowd. "So, I'd like for Taylor to come out and have her moment." The teen hugged Beyoncé and finished the acceptance speech Ye interrupted. When the pair walked offstage, MTV News correspondent Jim Cantiello was waiting in the wings to interview them. "No, no, no—I'm not doing press," Bey told him. "The person you're gonna want to talk to is coming down soon," she quipped about Taylor, who was "way more composed" than she had been following the incident, remembered Cantiello.

Bey's kind gesture was the beginning of a friendship between her and Taylor that was built on mutual respect. Fourteen years later in 2023, the superstars shattered records with their respective world tours—and showed up to celebrate each other's wins. Taylor slipped into a chrome gown for the London premiere of *Renaissance: A Film by Beyoncé*, while Bey joined the "Karma" singer on the red carpet at *The Eras Tour* concert film in Los Angeles. "I'm so glad I'll never know what my life would've been like without @Beyoncé's influence," Taylor captioned an Instagram photo of the two eating popcorn in the theater. "The way she's taught me and every artist out here to break rules and defy industry norms. Her generosity of spirit. Her resilience and versatility. She's been a guiding light throughout my career and the fact that she showed up tonight was like an actual fairytale."

DYNAMIC DUO

In 2010, two of the biggest pop stars on the planet—Beyoncé and Lady Gaga—joined forces for "Telephone," a collaboration so iconic that some say it paved the way for Bey to take more artistic risks. The big-budget video, which depicts the duo as murderous fashionistas, certainly revealed a different side of the singer as she emerged from her *Sasha Fierce* era. "Beyoncé, the most egregiously non-crazy pop star of our time, gets to pretend she's as nuts as Gaga for a few minutes," noted *Rolling Stone*.

The mini movie opens with Gaga in jail for killing her boyfriend, a storyline that originated in her "Paparazzi" video. She's eventually bailed out by Beyoncé, who picks her up in a pickup truck painted with flames, the same "Pussy Wagon" driven by Uma Thurman in Quentin Tarantino's *Kill Bill*. "You've been a very bad girl," purrs Bey, all glam in black lipstick and retro-pinup hair. In the next scene at a greasy diner, she's dressed to kill in head-to-toe yellow latex (with matching eye makeup). Not only does Bey pour poison into her abusive boyfriend's coffee, turns out Gaga slipped it into everyone's food—and once they all keel over, the two popstars dance among the bodies while decked out in patriotic stars-and-stripes ensembles. The ten-minute video, directed by Jonas Åkerlund (who worked with Bey on her "Haunted" and "Superpower" visuals), ends with the dynamic duo on the run from police à la *Thelma and Louise*. "To be continued . . ." flashes across the screen—yet fans are *still* waiting for the sequel.

With "Telephone," Gaga hoped to create something so edgy that MTV wouldn't want to air it on network television. Indeed, YouTube is where the video went viral, amassing 466 million views since its release. A decade later in 2020, the *New York Times* looked back at the video's

"Tonight I want you to stand up on your feet, I want you to feel the love that's growing inside of me."

impact: "'Telephone' remains one of the wildest and most watchable pop artifacts of its era, a defining moment in the music video's migration from MTV to the unruly internet."

OH, BABY

On Bey's 2011 "Countdown," she talks about trying to make her and Jay-Z a three. And two months after its release, she confirmed her pregnancy onstage at the *MTV Video Music Awards* as a record-breaking 12.4 million people watched from home. Introducing her performance of "Love on Top," Bey told the unsuspecting crowd, "Tonight I want you to stand up on your feet, I want you to feel the love that's growing inside of me." No one was the wiser until the end of the song when she dropped the mic—literally and figuratively—and unbuttoned her Dolce & Gabbana sequined blazer to reveal her baby bump hidden beneath.

The shock announcement spread like wildfire on Twitter (now known as X), garnering 8,868 posts per second, a new world record. Those who missed the breaking news broke the Internet: "Beyoncé pregnant" was the most searched term on Google over the following week. Five months later, she and Jay-Z welcomed their daughter, Blue Ivy.

Looking back on the iconic announcement in 2021, Tina Knowles revealed it had initially been "a stressful night." As her daughter's stylist, she was in panic mode two hours before stage time when the singer realized her pants were too tight around her growing belly. Tina rushed to the nearest A Pea in the Pod maternity clothing store and bought two new pairs, but they didn't fit either. With little time to spare, she cut out the stretch panel in one of the store-bought pants and stitched it into her custom design. "Thank God it worked," Tina revealed in an Instagram post celebrating the tenth anniversary. "When she opened that jacket and showed her stomach it was the biggest relief ever . . . We didn't have to keep the secret anymore . . . It was the best feeling in the world to [see] her show the whole world that tummy."

Later, Beyoncé found a creative new way to tell the world she was expecting twins. On February 1, 2017, she posted a high-art portrait of herself kneeling in front of a wall of flowers and cradling her belly with the caption "We have been blessed two times over." Within hours, it became the most liked Instagram post ever with 6.3 million reactions (as of 2024, it's hovering around eleven million). Bey held the title for 371 days, until getting bumped by Kylie Jenner's first photo of her daughter, Stormi.

SUPERBOWL SUPERPOWER

Beyoncé's 2013 Super Bowl halftime show brought the house down—and also the house lights, it seemed. Following her electrifying performance at the Mercedes-Benz Superdome in New Orleans, play resumed between the Baltimore Ravens and San Francisco 49ers, until moments into the third quarter when the stadium suddenly went black. As NFL officials scrambled to restore power for thirty-four minutes, the assumption was that Beyoncé had caused the outage. While football followers were annoyed, the BeyHive buzzed about the Queen's true power. "If you liked it, you should've put a backup generator on it," tweeted one fan. Even celebrities got in on the fun: "Beyoncé literally killed it at the Super Bowl," joked *The Tonight Show* host, Jimmy Fallon. "I don't think the Superdome was ready for that jelly . . ." added *Modern Family* star Sarah Hyland, referencing "Bootylicious."

CBS analyst Boomer Esiason claimed after Beyoncé's performance that he heard an "electrical buzz sound coming from the ceiling . . . And by the way, Beyoncé blew the electricity in the Superdome twice, I'm told, during her rehearsals during the week." However, the NFL was adamant in its defense of the singer. "There's no indication at all that this was caused by the halftime show. Absolutely none," Commissioner Roger Goodell insisted at a press conference. Superdome manager Doug Thornton also explained why Bey was innocent: "The halftime show was run on 100 percent generated power. That means it was not on our power grid at all."

BILLION DOLLARS IN AN ELEVATOR

Before she turned lemons into *Lemonade*, Beyoncé regained control of her family's narrative on the 2014 remix of "***Flawless." Three months

*Beyoncé literally killed it
at the Super Bowl.*

earlier, her private life was publicized when surveillance video from inside an elevator captured Bey's sister Solange screaming at Jay-Z and even taking a swing at him, yet his wife didn't intervene. According to reports, Solange was upset with the "99 Problems" rapper over something he said to her at the Met Gala afterparty, and once the elevator doors closed "she snapped." By the next morning, the incident was everywhere. The front pages of both the *New York Post* and *New York Daily News* splashed "Crazy-Z" across their front pages. That evening, Seth Meyers joked on *Late Night* that the video "brings Jay-Z's total to one hundred problems."

The trio released a joint statement acknowledging "the unfortunate incident." Solange and Jay-Z "have apologized to each other," they revealed, "and we have moved forward as a united family . . . At the end of the day, families have problems, and we're no different. We love each other, and above all, we are family. We've put this behind us and hope everyone else will do the same."

Beyoncé got the last word, with the remix of "***Flawless" featuring Nicki Minaj, which included a new verse about how it's only natural that things go down when there's a billion dollars in one elevator car. It was an uncharacteristically feisty Beyoncé—and it was a hit: dubbed the best song of 2014 by *Time*, the remix "reminded listeners of Beyoncé's innovative spirit."

MUTE CHALLENGE

Beyoncé concerts are a high-energy singalong, but for several seconds every night of the 2023 Renaissance Tour, she indirectly encouraged audiences to be completely silent. During performances of "Energy," immediately following the lyric that mentions muting everybody, the singer and her dancers froze in place—and hoped fans would too. However, the Mute Challenge didn't catch on immediately. Throughout the tour's early dates in Europe, audiences continued to sing the next line, even though Bey stood still gesturing "shhh" with her hand.

But as the global trek progressed, fans picked up on Bey's nonverbal cue and the Mute Challenge turned into a competition. Social media blew up with video clips of concertgoers shaming those who couldn't zip their lips during the moment of silence. After the Washington, D.C. show, the singer's website declared the nation's capital the "eerbody on mute war winner." But days later in Atlanta, she was so wowed that the seventy thousand in attendance stayed utterly silent for five whole seconds, she ad-libbed the next line, screaming, " Y'all won! Y'all won! Y'all won!"

BEY-TIONARY

Alkaline Wrist *noun: a wrist full of bracelets, an indication of one's wealth*

Beyoncé has boasted about being "iced up" with diamonds and sung about wanting "a ring on it," and on *Renaissance*'s "Thique," she coined new slang related to jewelry: alkaline wrist. As her body gets "thiquer" so does her cash flow—and her wealth affords her a wrist full of bracelets. During the Renaissance Tour, the full lyric was a popular photo caption on Instagram.

Boof-boof *noun: vehicle belonging to one's boo*

When Bey dropped "Countdown" back in 2011, no one could quite make out the pre-chorus line, with fans as well as journalists from *Rolling Stone*, *Entertainment Weekly*, and MTV News all questioning if they were hearing "me and my boof," "boof-boof ridin," or even "boo coup ridin." Ultimately, "boof-boof" stuck and the misinterpretation is widely considered to be a car in which two boos ride around town.

Bootylicious *adjective: voluptuously attractive, particularly in one's derriere*

Back in 2001, Destiny's Child asked if the listener could handle their bootylicious body. A combo of "booty" and "delicious," the chart-topping "Bootylicious" was officially added to the

Merriam-Webster dictionary in 2004—but it's not something Bey's "very proud of," she admitted to David Letterman two years later. "I wish there was another word I could have come up with if I was going to have a word in the dictionary."

Boy bye *phrase: dismissive send-off to a person who bothers you*
On "Sorry," Bey suggests that when you've had enough of a toxic person, "tell him, 'boy bye.'" The 2016 phrase from *Lemonade* quickly replaced the then-popular "Bye Felicia" from the 1995 comedy *Friday*, in which Ice Cube's character Craig literally bids goodbye to an annoying mooch named Felisha. "Boy bye" made it all the way to the Democratic National Committee, which adopted it for an anti-Donald Trump tweet ahead of the 2020 presidential election.

Getting Bodied *verb: to excite someone on the dancefloor to the point they want to get closer*
Beyoncé envisions a night out at the club in her sexiest dress—and her "mission" of successfully grabbing a man's attention and grinding on the dancefloor—in the female empowerment anthem, "Get Me Bodied," which she wrote with her sister, Solange, and cousin Angela Beyince. As she explains in the song, the verb means to bring a body closer until two bodies are touching.

H-Town *proper noun: Beyoncé's home town of Houston,*
the largest city in Texas
She didn't coin the nickname, but Bey certainly popularized
"H-Town" as a reference to Houston. On 2013's *Beyoncé*, she
name-checks the city twice, on "***Flawless" and "No Angel."
A decade later, when she brought out Megan Thee Stallion as
a surprise guest for the Renaissance Tour's stop in Houston, Bey
thanked "My H-Town sister" in a social media post.

I woke up like this *phrase: to awake from slumber in a*
state of perfection and glamour
Bey's empowerment anthem "***Flawless" not only influenced
people to use the title to describe their impeccable appearance,
but a lyric in its chorus became a viral photo caption. The
trend of posting an au naturel selfie accompanied by "I woke
up like this" also inspired parodies in which the subject looks
intentionally flawed. To this day, it's not uncommon to scroll
through Instagram and come across "I woke up like this": A
decade since Bey's hit single, the phrase has generated over
five million hashtags.

Put a ring on it *verb: to propose marriage to a*
worthy person
Bey gave the diamond industry free publicity in 2008 with her
No. 1 "Single Ladies," telling everyone everywhere to propose

to your loved one or someone else will. More than fifteen years later, newly engaged couples still use the timeless phrase to caption social media photos of their post-proposal moments, specifically a ring finger adorned with a diamond.

Slay *verb: to greatly impress or achieve success*
Sure, the word *slay* has been around since medieval times—commonly in reference to killing beasts, dragons, and vampires—but in 2016 Bey popularized a variation of the verb, "dressed to kill," that originated during the 1980s drag ballroom culture. The crossover into modern pop culture can be attributed to her *Lemonade* track "Formation," which encourages ladies to get in line and "slay all day." The superstar certainly does, which is why the BeyHive has coined "BeyonSlay" and "Slayoncé."

Surfbort *noun: a sexual position meant to take place in a bathtub*
On "Drunk in Love," an ode to husband Jay-Z, the singer provides quite a visual of what happens when she consumes too much of the rapper's Armand de Brignac champagne. A mispronunciation of *surfboard*, it describes a sexual position meant for the bathroom, not the bedroom. Similar to the actual water sport, the partner on top mimics riding a surfboard.

ECONOMIC
TRENDSETTER

As a global superstar, naturally Beyoncé has major influence—and her power has been surging for over two decades. In 2001, she signed her first contract with L'Oréal, worth $4.7 million, to promote the global cosmetics brand's Feria hair color and True Match foundation lines. Over the five-year deal, Bey convinced consumers "you're worth it." L'Oréal's operating profits increased by more than a billion dollars. It was the same exponential success for Pepsi. In 2002, Bey replaced Britney Spears as spokesperson, and after she starred in several TV commercials (by herself and opposite the likes of Britney, Jennifer Lopez, and David Beckham), PepsiCo's annual revenue boomed by at least $10 billion in 2007. All it took was the debut of a new song, "Standing on the Sun,"—and Bey rocking a bikini—for her 2013 H&M swimwear collaboration to heat up the clothing retailer's annual sales by $26 million. Several brands have learned that a lyrical namedrop from Queen Bey is a priceless endorsement. In 2016, not only did her sixth album boost the popularity of lemonade (which had been steadily dwindling since 2004), but the mere mention of taking her man to Red Lobster in "Formation" increased sales at the seafood restaurant chain by 33 percent. On her next album, the stylish singer dubbed Telfar the new It Bag (and revealed Birkins were out of style) in "Summer Renaissance." The free advertising paid off for the up-and-coming New York designer, whose affordable vegan Shopping Bag sold out online. Fans then flocked to the designer resale site The RealReal, where views of Telfar items spiked 85 percent in one day.

Cities around the world have also felt "The Beyoncé Effect" (often referred to as "Beyoncé Bump" and "Beyflation"), a term describing her influence over market trends. Every stop on her 2023 Renaissance Tour translated to big revenue for local businesses, from hotels and restaurants to salons and limousine rentals. In the US, Beyoncé contributed $4.5 billion to the economy by the time she took a bow at her final show in Kansas City, according to the *New York Times*. For comparison, that's equivalent to the economic impact of the 2008 Olympics in Beijing—proof that Bey always goes for the gold. "This is so awesome," gushed proud mother Tina Knowles on social media. "To [be] able to stimulate the economy is no small feat!"

Ahead of each concert, fans turned to Yelp for recommendations on where to eat, drink, shop, get their hair done (and their nails done, too). "Beyoncé is a force, and it's fascinating to see the level of excitement and tangible interest generated for the local shops and businesses," said Yelp's trend expert, Tara Lewis. "Whether it's people looking for dining and nightlife options, getting glammed up, or booking transportation, the 'Beyoncé Bump' is real, and it's helping more people connect with local businesses in their communities." Small businesses owned by Black people, women, and LGBTQ+ people especially felt the financial sunbeams of Beyoncé. Ahead of her first US show in Philadelphia, consumer interest increased in three categories: Black-owned beauty, LGBTQ+, and women-owned shopping. "Everyone wants to look their best for Queen Bey," reasoned Lewis.

Entrepreneurs found new and creative ways to cater to the BeyHive. In Atlanta—where small businesses collectively earned $10 million in revenue—fans could order the Queen's Lemonade, with slow-brewed hibiscus tea and edible glitter, at Peoples Town Coffee; silver buttercream sweets, complete with a mini disco ball, were available at Trophy Cupcakes in Seattle; and the Houston Humane Society in the singer's hometown waived adoption fees for "thique" dogs weighing over forty pounds in honor of the popular *Renaissance* track. Elsewhere across the US, there were Beyoncé-themed dance parties, drag brunches, yoga sessions, and even cake-making classes.

FINE ARTIST

Beyoncé is a woman of many hidden talents: She can tie a cherry stem with her tongue, flare her nose in two different places, and beat anyone in a game of Connect Four. But perhaps the most intriguing skill is the one she keeps to herself: She can paint. She began with portraits of women, using oil paints because that's the most challenging medium. "I got hooked and wouldn't sleep . . . I made this special room with saris and pillows. I would light candles, play Miles Davis and Björk, and paint all night," Bey told journalist James Patrick Herman. "It was therapeutic. Whenever I finish one of my paintings, I try to figure out what it represents in my life. I'll be like, 'It's dark behind her and light in front of her, so a dark period must be coming to an end. Something light and beautiful is going to happen.'"

However, fans shouldn't expect a peek at her works of art any time soon. "I've never shown anyone any of my paintings except my mom and my family," Bey told ABC News. But her close circle got a front row seat to her talent at a birthday party for Bey's producer, Swizz Beatz, thrown by his wife, Alicia Keys. "We had canvases everywhere and you did whatever you could—even if you could only splat paint on it," recalled the "Girl on Fire" singer. "Beyoncé's actually a really beautiful painter."

She inherited her appreciation of art from Tina Knowles, a longtime collector, who taught her daughter about the importance of investing in art. Beyoncé and Jay-Z, one of the wealthiest couples in the world, have shelled out a reported $70 million for one-of-a-kind pieces from Andy Warhol, Jean-Michel Basquiat, Damien Hirst, Marilyn Minter, Richard Prince, and David Hammons. However, a black-and-white photograph by Laurie Simmons is actually a replacement. Jay-Z revealed to *Rolling Stone* in 2010 that he originally purchased "Walking Gun," a provocative snapshot of a pistol with a pair of women's legs as the handle, but Bey sent it back in favor of a more feminine image featuring a perfume bottle. The Carters' private collection even has its very own museum: their $200 million home in Malibu, specifically designed to showcase the previous owner's pricey pieces. The mansion itself is a work of art, modeled after the Pulitzer Arts Foundation museum in St. Louis, Missouri, and built by the same architect, Tadao Ando.

Bey and Jay are fixtures on the art scene, visiting galleries and museums in cities all over the world. In New York City, the couple got a preview of Sadie Barnette's 2017 exhibit *Compland,* with art created based on the five-hundred-page FBI surveillance file on her father, Rodney Barnette, founder of the Compton chapter of the Black Panthers. In Los Angeles, they were two of the famous faces who checked out the 2019 Frieze International Art Fair. During the 2023 Renaissance Tour's stop in St. Louis, Jay-Z stopped by the Pulitzer to see Richard Serra's thirteen-foot-tall (4 m) spiral steel sculpture, "Joe." For their 2018 side project, *The Carters,* the duo rented out the Louvre in Paris to shoot the "Apeshit" video. The artsy six-minute clip highlights some of the most notable works in history, including Leonardo da Vinci's "Mona Lisa," the 150 BCE sculpture "Venus de Milo," and Marie-Guillemine Benoist's oil painting "Portrait of a Black Woman" from 1800.

Basquiat, who rose to fame in the 1980s for his Neo-Expressionist street art, is one of Bey's favorites, along with Pop artist Keith Haring, minimalist Donald Judd, contemporary painters Kara Walker and Aaron Young, and installation artist Tracey Emin. But her first true love was the classics. "When I was twenty years old, I visited the Sistine Chapel and saw Michelangelo's work and it was one of the most spectacular experiences of my life," Bey gushed to *Harper's Bazaar* in 2011. "I then went on a tour around Europe and visited all the places where Picasso and Matisse hung out. I then visited Art Basel [in Miami] and was exposed to all kinds of contemporary artists. It got me into art that's more abstract. Art inspires me in so many ways. I use art as a reference when I'm looking for inspiration for my performances, wardrobe, or a video I might be working on."

VISUAL
STORYTELLER

G ifted with an artistic eye, Beyoncé can not only visualize what she wants her projects to look like, she has the tools to bring it to life herself. The singer has directed several of her documentaries, visual albums, and concert films, starting with 2010's I Am . . . World Tour. The year prior, Bey learned how to use Final Cut Pro (a professional video-editing app) and after coming off the road, she spent nine months editing endless hours of footage. A combination of performances and backstage moments, the DVD gave fans a 360-degree look at the superstar's life—and within four weeks it became the year's best-selling video album worldwide. "It was the beginning of a newfound love and creative expression," Bey told *Harper's Bazaar*.

And it inspired her to raise her own expectations. Afterwards, Bey took on an autobiographical television film, *Life Is But a Dream*, for HBO. Since 2005, a visual director had been documenting her every waking moment—as much as sixteen hours a day—and in 2012 it was time to piece it all together. The singer spent the better part of a year in the cutting room telling her own story, which included intimate glimpses of her relationship with Jay-Z (in one clip, the couple sings Coldplay's "Yellow" to each other over dinner) as well as her heartbreaking miscarriage before welcoming Blue Ivy in 2012. "That was important to me," Bey revealed to *The Gentlewoman*. "I was really, really careful about the editing and making sure it was told in an elegant way. I felt like, kind of, it's time. But it was very important that it was not about me being a singer or an entertainer. At the end of the day, it's a story about being a woman overcoming the struggles and keeping on trucking." The content was clearly riveting: *Life Is But a Dream* drew 2.3 million viewers, the largest audience for an HBO documentary.

After orchestrating two visual albums, *Beyoncé* and *Lemonade*, she brought fans behind the scenes once again with *Homecoming*, a concert film documenting her 2018 Coachella performance and "the emotional road from creative concept to cultural movement," according to Netflix, which signed Bey to a $60 million three-project deal. Written, executive-produced, and directed by Beyoncé, *Homecoming* peeled back the curtain of how she prepared for her first performance since giving birth to twins Rumi and Sir—while also being a present mother to her three children. "What people don't see is the sacrifice," she says in the film. "I definitely pushed myself further than I knew I could. And I learned a very valuable lesson. I will never, never push myself that far again." The effort was appreciated and admired: *Homecoming* was nominated for six Primetime Emmy Awards and won Best Music Film at the 2020 *Grammys*.

That year, she released her third visual album, *Black Is King*, the companion to *The Lion King: The Gift*, which contained curated songs inspired by the 2019 remake. A passion project, it was also a labor of love. Bey spent a solid year researching, writing, filming, and editing the musical film about an exiled African prince's journey to reclaiming his throne. "It started out simple, in my backyard. I wanted to do one or two videos for *The Gift* album, then it just grew," she explained to British *Vogue*. "Before we knew it, we were shooting in Nigeria, Ghana, London, Los Angeles, Johannesburg, and KwaZulu-Natal, South Africa, where we filmed with the women of the Himba tribe." *Black Is King*, which streamed on Disney+, won a Primetime Emmy for its costume design which featured sixty-nine pieces created by Beyoncé herself.

Bey got back to basics with 2023's *Renaissance: A Film by Beyoncé*. The singer wrote, produced, and directed the documentary concert film that went behind the scenes of her world tour. Exclusively distributed by AMC Theatres, *Renaissance* earned $22 million on its first weekend, the second-best opening since Tom Cruise's *The Last Samurai* in 2003. "It was one of the hardest things I've ever done because of the short turnaround time," Bey told fans on Instagram. "I practically slept in the edit, color, and mix sessions. The race against time continued in order to get this film out so quickly. But it was so worth all the grind."

CHARITABLE
SOUL

Since she was nine, Beyoncé has been lending a helpful hand to charity, starting with local homeless shelters in Houston. As her career took off, she continued to give back—and broaden her reach. After donating money to underprivileged youth and Hurricane Katrina survivors, the singer-actress gave her entire $4 million paycheck from *Cadillac Records* to Phoenix House, a drug and alcohol rehabilitation center where she spent time preparing for her role as Etta James, who struggled with heroin addiction.

But when she turned thirty, she found herself wanting to dig deeper into life—and that included working to improve the world around her. In 2013, she launched BeyGOOD, a foundation that focuses on global matters such as disaster relief, education, housing, mental health, and economic equity. "From scholarships to the water crisis in Burundi to helping families during Hurricane Harvey in my hometown, Houston, it has been beyond fulfilling to be of service," Beyoncé said in a 2023 statement commemorating a decade of BeyGOOD. "Now, as a foundation, we will continue the work of engaging partners through innovative programs to impact even more people."

DISASTER RELIEF

Bey's first international mission came in 2015, when she traveled to Haiti to check on the rebuild progress made in the five years since a magnitude 7.0 earthquake devastated the impoverished Caribbean country and killed an estimated 300,000 people. At the Saint Damien Pediatric Hospital, she visited young cancer patients, bringing smiles to their faces and passing out toys. The BeyGOOD T-shirt she wore was highly publicized—and for good reason: it was available for purchase on her charity's website, with all proceeds going directly to the hospital.

Two years later, when Hurricane Harvey impacted her hometown, Beyoncé specifically organized BeyGOOD Houston to restore the city both temporarily and for the long term. Blankets, pillows, cots, baby essentials, and feminine products were distributed along with four hundred meals sponsored by the singer, who personally served the displaced survivors alongside her daughter Blue Ivy and Destiny's Child bandmate Michelle Williams. "My heart goes out to my hometown," Bey told the *Houston*

Chronicle, "and I remain in constant prayer for those affected and for the rescuers who have been so brave and determined to do so much to help." After Florida was hit by back-to-back hurricanes in 2022, BeyGOOD was there to offer assistance. In partnership with Adidas and Amazon, the foundation provided necessities to those impacted—as well as several $5,000 grants to Black-owned small businesses.

EDUCATIONAL EQUITY

Empowerment has always been a tenet of Bey's philosophy, and with BeyGOOD she put focus on the advancement of young people. In 2017, she celebrated the anniversary of *Lemonade* with the Formation Scholars Program, which awarded $25,000 to four female college students studying creative arts, music, literature, and African American studies. Following her historic Coachella headlining in 2018—which spotlighted Historically Black Colleges and Universities—she announced the Homecoming Scholars Award Program for the 2018–2019 academic year to benefit four students from HBCU higher education institutions Xavier, Wilberforce, Tuskegee, and Bethune-Cookman. Bey then upped the ante even more for her highly anticipated 2023 tour with a $1 million Renaissance Scholarship Fund, which pledged $100,000 endowments for each of the ten HBCUs to disperse among selected beneficiaries.

COVID-19 RELIEF

In 2020, as the coronavirus paralyzed American communities, BeyGOOD sprang into action, teaming up with local organizations to distribute food, water, cleaning supplies, and face masks. Beyoncé also pledged $6 million to provide mental health and personal wellness services to

"I am doing
what my family has always done
in celebrating and uplifting
the Black community."

essential workers nationwide. In Houston, she donated COVID-19 tests, gloves, masks, vitamins, and grocery vouchers. "I try to think of the most productive way I can help," she told British *Vogue*. "It was heartwarming to see the photos from the testing sites and to read the letters from the people who were high-risk due to pre-existing health conditions, who were able to recover and return home safely from the hospital." Additionally, she hopped on the remix of Megan Thee Stallion's "Savage" and both Houstonians graciously granted the proceeds of their No. 1 hit to Bread of

Life, Houston's COVID-19 relief efforts. Looking back at one of the darkest periods in modern history, Bey summed up 2020 to *Vogue*: "It's been a year of service for me."

BLACK AMERICANS

Through BeyGOOD and on her own, Beyoncé has prioritized aiding and elevating Black Americans. In 2015, amid racial unrest in Baltimore and Ferguson, she and her husband Jay-Z donated tens of thousands to help bail out Black Lives Matter protestors who were arrested while taking a stand. The following year, the couple gave another $1.5 million to several civil rights groups, including BLM and Hands Up United.

But as injustice raged on, so did their work. In 2020, Beyoncé not only spoke out on the murder of George Floyd by a white police officer, but she also put her money where her mouth is with "Black Parade," a charity single celebrating Black culture. All proceeds went to the BeyGOOD Black Business Impact Fund to support those negatively affected by the protests—and within six months, $7.15 million had been distributed. The next phase was the Black Parade Route, which followed along on the 2023 Renaissance Tour. In select cities such as Chicago, Atlanta, and Houston, local Black entrepreneurs were invited to BeyGOOD events offering support services for business sustainability. By the end of Beyoncé's tour, $1 million in grants had been provided to one thousand small businesses on the Black Parade Route.

"I am doing what my family has always done in celebrating and uplifting the Black community," Beyoncé told British *Vogue*. "I've spent a lot of time focusing on building my legacy and representing my culture the best way I know how."

First published in 2024 by Epic Ink, an imprint of The Quarto Group,
142 West 36th Street, 4th Floor, New York, NY 10018, USA
(212) 779-4972 www.Quarto.com

Epic Ink titles are also available at discount for retail, wholesale, promotional, and bulk purchase. For details, contact the Special Sales Manager by email at specialsales@quarto.com or by mail at The Quarto Group, Attn: Special Sales Manager, 100 Cummings Center Suite 265D, Beverly, MA 01915 USA.

10 9 8 7 6 5 4 3 2 1

ISBN: 978-0-7603-9313-0

Digital edition published in 2024
eISBN: 978-0-7603-9314-7

Library of Congress Cataloging-in-Publication Data

Names: Perricone, Kathleen, author.
Title: Beyonce is life : a superfan's guide to all things we love about
   Beyonce / Kathleen Perricone.
Description: New York : Epic Ink, 2024. | Summary: "Beyoncé Is Life is a
   beautifully illustrated guide that explores and celebrates the singer
   and her music"-- Provided by publisher.
Identifiers: LCCN 2024009879 (print) | LCCN 2024009880 (ebook) | ISBN
   9780760393130 (hardcover) | ISBN 9780760393147 (ebook)
Subjects: LCSH: Beyoncé, 1981- | Singers--United States--Biography. |
   LCGFT: Biographies.
Classification: LCC ML420.K675 P47 2024 (print) | LCC ML420.K675 (ebook)
   | DDC 782.42164092 [B]--dc23/eng/20240301
LC record available at https://lccn.loc.gov/2024009879
LC ebook record available at https://lccn.loc.gov/2024009880

Group Publisher: Rage Kindelsperger
Senior Acquiring Editor: Nicole James
Creative Director: Laura Drew
Managing Editor: Cara Donaldson
Editors: Sara Bonacum and Katelynn Abraham
Cover and Interior Design: Beth Middleworth
Book Layout: Danielle Smith-Boldt
Illustrations: Kelly Smith

Printed in China

ACKNOWLEDGMENTS

As a Beyoncé fan dating back to the Destiny's Child days, I've had the privilege of witnessing her evolution into the most innovative musical artist of our time. Writing this book, I got to look back at the journey thus far—every multiplatinum album, every Grammy, every culture shift—and it's resounding: She is one of one, No. 1 . . . the only one.

Thank you, Beyoncé, for sacrificing so much of yourself for your fans. And thank you to the BeyHive for encouraging me to dig even deeper to tell her extraordinary story.

ABOUT THE AUTHOR

Kathleen Perricone is a biographer with published titles about Marilyn Monroe, John F. Kennedy, Anne Frank, Barack Obama, Taylor Swift, Harry Styles, and dozens more. Over the past two decades, Kathleen has also worked as a celebrity news editor in New York City as well as for Yahoo!, Ryan Seacrest Productions, and a reality TV family who shall remain nameless. She lives in Los Angeles.